THE SCHOOL BY THE SEA

BY

ANGELA BRAZIL

ANGELA BRAZIL

CHAPTER I

The Interloper

GIRLS! Girls everywhere! Girls in the passages, girls in the hall, racing upstairs and scurrying downstairs, diving into dormitories and running into classrooms, overflowing on to the landing and hustling along the corridor—everywhere, girls! There were tall and short, and fat and thin, and all degrees from pretty to plain; girls with fair hair and girls with dark hair, blue-eyed, brown-eyed, and grey-eyed girls; demure girls, romping girls, clever girls, stupid girls—but never a silent girl. No! Buzz-hum-buzz! The talk and chatter surged in a full, steady flow round the house till the noise invaded even that sanctuary of sanctuaries, the private study, where Miss Birks, the Principal, sat addressing post cards to inform respective parents of the safe arrival of the various individual members of the frolicsome crew which had just reassembled after the Christmas vacation. In ordinary circumstances such an indiscretion as squealing on the stairs or dancing in the passages would have brought Miss Birks from her den, dealing out stern rebukes, if not visiting dire justice on the offenders; but for this one brief evening—the first night of the term—the old house was Liberty Hall. Each damsel did what seemed good in her own eyes, and talked, laughed, and joked to her heart's content.

"Let them fizz, poor dears!" said Miss Birks, smiling to herself as a special outburst of mirth was wafted up from below. "It does them good to work off steam when they arrive. They'll have to be quiet enough to-morrow. Really, the twenty make noise enough for a hundred! They're all on double-voice power to-night! Shades of the Franciscans, what a noise! It seems almost sacrilege in an old convent."

If indeed the gentle, grey-robed nuns who long, long ago had stolen silently along those very same stairs could have come back to survey the scene of their former activities, I fear on this particular occasion they would have wrung their slim, transparent hands in horror over the stalwart modern maidens who had succeeded them in possession of the ancient, rambling house. No pale-faced novices these, with downcast eyes and cheeks sunken with fasting; no timid glances, no soft ethereal footfalls or gliding garments—the old order had changed indeed, and yielded place to a rosy, racy, healthy, hearty, well-grown set of twentieth-century schoolgirls, overflowing with vigorous young life and abounding spirits, mentally and physically fit, and about as different from their mediaeval forerunners as a hockey stick is from a spindle.

Among the jolly, careless company that on this January evening held carnival in the vaulted passages, and woke the echoes of the time-hallowed walls, no two had abandoned themselves to the fun of the moment more thoroughly than Deirdre Sullivan and Dulcie Wilcox. They had attempted to dance five varieties of fancy steps on an upper landing, had performed a species of Highland fling down the stairs, and had finished with an irregular jog-trot along the lower corridor, subsiding finally, scarlet with their exertions, and wellnigh voiceless, on to the bottom step of the back staircase.

"Oh!—let's—sit here—and talk," heaved Deirdre, her power of speech returning in jerks. "I'm—tired—of ragging round—and—I've not seen you—for ages!—and oh!—there's such heaps and heaps—to tell. Look! —she's over there!"

"Who?" queried Dulcie laconically. She was stouter than Deirdre, and, like Hamlet, "scant of breath".

"Why, she, of course!"

"Don't be a lunatic! Which she? And what she? And why she of all shes?" gasped Dulcie, still rather convulsively and painfully.

"What 'she' could I possibly mean except the new girl?"

"You don't mean to tell me there's a new girl?"

"You don't surely mean to tell me you've never noticed her! You blind bat! Why, there she is as large as life! Can't you see her, stupid? The atrocious part of it is, she's been stuck into our bedroom!"

Dulcie sprang up, with hands outstretched in utter tragedy.

"No!" she wailed, "oh, no! no! Surely Miss Birks hasn't been heartless enough to fill up that spare bed! Oh, I'll never forgive her, never! Our ducky, chummy little room to be invaded by a third—and a stranger! It's sheer barbarous cruelty! Oh, I thought better of her! What have we done to be treated like this? It's pure and simple brutality!"

"Who's the lunatic now? Stop ranting, you goose! That bed was bound to be filled some day, though it's hard luck on us. We did pretty well to keep the place to ourselves the whole of last term. 'All good things come to an end.' I'm trying to be philosophical, and quote proverbs; all the same, 'Two's company and three's a crowd'. That's a proverb too! You haven't told me yet what you think of our number three. She's talking to Mademoiselle over there."

"So she is! Why, if she isn't talking German, too, as pat as a native! What a tremendous rate their tongues are going at it! I can't catch a single word. Is she a foreigner? She doesn't somehow quite suggest English by the look of her, does she?"

The new girl in question, the interloper who was to form the unwelcome third, and spoil the delightful *scène à deux* hitherto so keenly enjoyed by the chums, certainly had a rather un-British aspect when viewed even by impartial eyes. Her pink-and-white colouring, blue eyes, and her very fair flaxen hair were distinctly Teutonic; the cut of her dress, the shape of her shoes, the tiny satchel slung by a strap round her shoulder and under one arm—so unmistakably German in type—the enamelled locket bearing the Prussian Eagle on a blue ground, all showed a slightly appreciable difference from her companions, and stamped her emphatically with the seal and signet of the "Vaterland". On the whole she might be considered a decidedly pretty girl; her features were small and clear cut, her complexion beyond reproach, her teeth even, her fair hair glossy, and she was moderately tall for her fifteen years.

Dulcie took in all these points with a long, long comprehensive stare, then subsided on to the top of the boot rack, shaking her head gloomily.

"You may call it British prejudice, but I can't stand foreigners," she remarked with a gusty sigh. "As for having one in one's bedroom—why, it's wicked! Miss Birks oughtn't to expect it!"

"Foreigners? Who's talking about foreigners?" asked Marcia Richards, one of the Sixth Form, who happened to be passing at the moment, and overheard Dulcie's complaints. "If you mean Gerda Thorwaldson, she is as English as you or I."

"English! Listen to her! Pattering German thirteen to the dozen!" snorted Dulcie.

"You young John Bull! Don't be insular and ridiculous! Gerda has lived in Germany, so of course she can speak German. It will be very good practice for you to talk it with her in your bedroom."

"If you think we're going to break our jaws with those abominable gutturals!"—broke out Deirdre.

"Miss Germany'll have to compass English, or hold her tongue," added Dulcie.

"Don't be nasty! You're wasting your opportunities. If I had your chance, I'd soon improve my German."

"Why didn't Miss Birks put her with you instead?" chimed the injured pair in chorus. "You're welcome to our share of her."

"Come along, you slackers!" interrupted Evie Bennett and Annie Pridwell, emerging from the dining-hall. "You're wasting time here. Betty Scott's playing for all she's worth, and everybody's got to come and dance. Pass the word on if anyone's upstairs. Are you ready? Hurry up, then!"

"Oh, I say! I'm tired!" yawned Dulcie.

"We've had enough of the light fantastic toe!" protested Deirdre.

"Little birds that can hop and won't hop must be made to hop!" chirped Evie firmly.

"How'll you make us?"

"The 'Great Mogul' has decreed that any girl who refuses to dance shall be forcibly placed upon the table and obliged to sing a solo, or forfeit all the sweets she may have brought back with her."

"'Tis Kismet!" murmured Deirdre, hauling up Dulcie from the boot rack.

"No use fighting against one's fate!" sighed Dulcie, linking arms with her chum as she walked along the passage.

After all, it was only the younger members who were assembled in the dining-hall—the Sixth, far too superior to join in the general romping, were having a select cocoa party in the head girl's bedroom, and telling each other that the noise below was disgraceful, and they wondered Miss Birks didn't put a stop to it. (At seventeen one's judgment is apt to be severe, especially on those only a few years younger!) Miss Birks, however, who was forty-five, and wise in her generation, did not interfere, and the fun downstairs continued to effervesce. Betty Scott, seated at the piano, played with skill and zeal, and the others were soon tripping their steps with more or less effect, according to their individual grace and agility—all but two. Hilda Marriott had strained her ankle during the holidays, and could only sit on the table and sigh with envy; while Gerda Thorwaldson, the new girl, stood by the door, watching the performance. Everybody was so taken up by the joys of the moment that nobody realized her presence, even when whirling skirts whisked against her in passing. Not a single one noticed her forlorn aloofness, or that the blue eyes were almost brimming over with tears. Mademoiselle, the only person who had so far befriended her, had beaten a retreat, and was finishing unpacking, while the fourteen fellow pupils in the room were still entire strangers to her. As nobody made the slightest overture towards an introduction, and she seemed rather in the way of the dancers, Gerda opened the door, and was about to follow Mademoiselle's example, and make her escape upstairs. Her action, however, attracted the attention that had before been denied her.

"Hallo, the new girl's sneaking off!" cried Annie Pridwell, pausing so suddenly that she almost upset her partner.

"Here! Stop!"

"Where are you going?"

"You've got to stay."

"Come here and report yourself!"

The dancing had come to a brief and sudden end. Betty Scott, concluding in the middle of a bar, turned round on the music stool, and holding up a commanding finger, beckoned the stranger forward.

"Let's have a look at you," she remarked patronizingly. "I hadn't time to take you in before. Are you really German? Tell us about yourself."

"Yes, go on! Where do you come from, and all the rest of it?" urged Evie Bennett.

"Are you dumb?" asked Rhoda Wilkins.

"Perhaps she can't speak English!" sniggered Dulcie Wilcox.

Gerda Thorwaldson, now the target of every eye, had turned crimson to the very roots of her flaxen hair. She stood in the centre of a ring of new schoolfellows, so overwhelmed with shyness that she did not volunteer a single response to the volley of remarks suddenly fired at her. This did not at all content her inquisitors, who, once their attention was drawn to her, felt their curiosity aroused.

"I say, why can't you speak?" said Barbara Marshall, nudging her elbow. "You needn't look so scared. We're not going to eat you!"

"No cannibals here!" piped Romola Harvey.

"Lost, stolen, or strayed—a tongue! The property of the new girl. Finder will be handsomely rewarded," remarked Mary Beckett facetiously.

"You've got to answer some questions, Gerda Thorwaldson—I suppose that's your name?—so don't be silly!" urged Irene Jordan.

"Speak up! We shan't stand any nonsense!" added Elyned Hughes.

"What do you want me to say?" murmured Gerda, gulping down her embarrassment with something suspiciously like a sob, and blinking her blue eyes rapidly.

"Oh, you can talk English! Well, to begin with, are you German or not?"

"No."

"But you come from Germany?"

"Yes."

"Have you ever been in Cornwall before?"

"Never."

"I suppose you can dance?"

"No."

At this last negative a united howl went up from the assembled circle.

"Can't dance? Where have you lived? Make her try! She's got to learn! Take her arm and teach her some steps! She won't? She'll have to! No one's to be let off to-night!"

"Gerda Thorwaldson," said Evie Bennett impressively, "we give you your choice. You either try to dance this very instant, or you stand on that table and sing a song—in English, mind, not German!"

"Which will you choose?" clamoured three or four urgent voices.

"Oh, I say! It's too bad to rag her so, just at first!" protested Doris Patterson, a shade more sympathetic than the rest.

"Not a bit of it! If she's really English, she must show it—and if she won't, she's nothing but a foreigner!" blustered Dulcie Wilcox.

"This is easy enough," volunteered Annie Pridwell, performing a few steps by way of encouragement. "Now, come along and do as I do."

"Fly, little birdie, fly!" mocked Betty Scott.

"She's too stupid!"

"She's going to blub!"

"Leave her alone!"

"No, make her dance!"

"Don't let her sneak out of it!"

"I say, what's going on here?" said a fresh voice, as Marcia Richards entered the room, and, after pausing a moment to take in the situation, strode indignantly to the rescue of poor Gerda, who, still shy and half-bewildered with so many questions, stood almost weeping in the midst of the circle.

"Is this the way you treat a new girl? You ought to be ashamed of yourselves! No, she shan't learn to dance if she doesn't want to! Not to-night, at any rate. Come along with me, Gerda, and have some cocoa upstairs. Don't trouble your head about this noisy set. If they've no better manners, I'm sorry for them!"

With which parting shot, she seized her protégée by the arm and bore her out of the room.

Most of the girls laughed. They did not take the affair seriously. A fit of bashfulness and blushing might be very agonizing to the new-comer, but it was distinctly diverting to outsiders. New girls must expect a little wholesome catechizing before they were admitted into the bosom of their Form. It was merely a species of initiation, nothing more. No doubt Gerda would find her tongue to-morrow, and give a better account of herself. So Betty sat down again to the piano, and the others, finding their partners, began once more to tread the fascinating steps of the latest popular dance.

"We did rag her, rather," said Deirdre half-apologetically.

"Serve her jolly well right for talking German!" snapped Dulcie.

CHAPTER II

A Kingdom by the Sea

PLEASE do not think because Miss Birks's pupils, on the first night of a new term, ran helter-skelter up and down the passages, and insisted on compulsory dancing or solo singing, that this was their normal course of procedure. It was but their one evening of liberty before they settled down to ordinary school routine, and for the rest of the eighty-eight days before Easter their behaviour would be quite exemplary.

They were a very happy little community at the Dower House. They admired and respected their headmistress, and her well-framed rules were rarely transgressed. Certainly the girls would have been hard to please if they had not been satisfied with Miss Birks, for allied to her undoubted brain power she had those far rarer gifts of perfect tact and absolute sympathy. She thoroughly understood that oft-time riddle, the mind of a schoolgirl, and, while still keeping her authority and maintaining the dignity of her position, could win her pupils' entire confidence almost as if she had been one of themselves.

"Miss Birks never seems to have quite grown up! She enjoys things just the same as we do," was the general verdict of the school.

Perhaps a strain of Irish in her genealogy had given the Principal the pleasant twinkle in her eye, the racy humour of speech, and the sunny optimistic view of life so dearly valued by all who knew her. Anyhow, whatever ancestry might claim to be the source of her cheery attributes, she had a very winning personality, and ruled her small kingdom with a hand so light that few realized its firmness. And a kingdom it was, in the girls' opinion—a veritable "kingdom by the sea". No place in all the length and breadth of the British Isles, so they considered, could in any way compare with it. Together with the old castle, for which it formed the Dower House, it stood on the neck of a long narrow peninsula that stretched for about two miles seaward. All the land on this little domain was the private property of Mrs. Trevellyan, the owner of Pontperran Tower, from whom Miss Birks rented the school, and who had granted full and entire leave for the pupils to wander where they wished. The result of this generous concession was to give the girls a much larger amount of freedom than would have been possible in any other situation. The isolated position of the peninsula, only accessible through the Castle gateway, made it as safe and secluded a spot as a convent garden, and afforded a range of scenery that might well be a source of congratulation to those who enjoyed it.

There are few schools that possess a whole headland for a playground, and especially such a headland, that seemed so completely equipped for the purpose. It held the most delightful of narrow coves, with gently shelving, sandy beaches—ideal bathing places in summer-time—and mysterious caverns that might occasionally be explored with a candle, and interesting pools among the rocks, where at low tide could be found seaweeds and anemones, and crabs and limpets, or a bestranded starfish. On the steep cliffs that rose sheer and jagged from the green water the seabirds built in the spring; and at the summit, on the very verge of the precipice, bloomed in their season many choice and rare wild flowers— the lovely vernal squill, with its blossoms like deep-blue stars; the handsome crimson crane's-bill; the yellow masses of the "Lady's fingers"; the pink tufts of the rosy thrift; or the fleshy leaves of the curious samphire. The whole extent of the headland was occupied by a tract of rough, heathery ground, generally called "the warren". A few sheep were turned out here to crop the fine grass that grew between the gorse bushes, and a pair of goats were often tethered within easy reach of the coachman's cottage; but otherwise it was the reserve of the rabbits that scuttled away in every direction should a human footstep invade the sanctuary of their dominion.

On these delightful breezy uplands, where the pleasant west wind blew fresh and warm from the Gulf Stream, Miss Birks's pupils might wander at will during play hours, only observing a few sensible restrictions. Dangerous climbs on the edge of the cliffs or over slippery rocks were forbidden, and not less than three girls must always be together. This last rule was a very necessary one in the circumstances, for in case of any accident to a member of the trio, it allowed one to stay with the sufferer and render any first aid possible, while the other went at topmost speed to lodge information at head-quarters.

The old dwelling itself was a suitable and appropriate building for a school. Erected originally in the fourteenth century as a small nunnery, it had in the days of Edward VI fallen into the hands of the then lord of the Castle, who had turned it into a dower house. Successive generations of owners had in their time added to it or altered it, but had not spoilt its general atmosphere of mediaevalism. Little pieces of Perpendicular window tracery, or remains of archways were frequent in the old walls, and a ruined turreted gateway bore witness to the beauty of the ancient architecture. Nobody quite knew what vaults and cellars there might be under the house. Remains of blocked-up staircases had certainly been found, and many of the floors resounded with a suggestively hollow ring; but all tradition of these had been lost, and not even a legend lingered to gratify the curious.

There was one element of mystery, however, which formed a perennial interest and a never-ending topic of conversation among the girls. In the centre of the first landing, right in the midst of the principal bedrooms, stood a perpetually-closed room. The heavy oak door was locked, and as an extra protection thick iron bars had been placed across and secured firmly to the jambs. Even the keyhole was stopped up, so that the most inquisitive eye could obtain no satisfaction. All that anybody knew was the fact that Mrs. Trevellyan, who had a well-deserved reputation for eccentricity, had caused a special clause to be made in the lease which she had granted to Miss Birks, stipulating for no interference with the barred room under pain of forfeiture of the entire agreement.

"That means if we bored a hole through the door and peeped in the whole school would be turned out of the house," said Evie Bennett once when the subject was under discussion.

"Even Miss Birks doesn't know what's inside," said Elyned Hughes with an awed shudder.

"Mrs. Trevellyan wouldn't let the place on any other conditions. She said she'd rather have it empty first," added Annie Pridwell.

"What can she have there?"

"I'd give ten thousand pounds to find out!"

But though speculation might run rife in the school and a hundred different theories be advanced, there was not the slightest means of verifying a single one of them. Ghosts, smugglers, or a family skeleton were among the favourite suggestions, and the girls often amused themselves with even wilder fancies. From the outside the secluded room presented as insuperable a barrier as from within; heavy shutters secured the window and guarded the secret closely and jealously from all prying and peeping. That uncanny noises should apparently issue from this abode of mystery goes without saying. There were mice in plenty, and even an occasional rat or two in the old house, and their gnawings, scamperings, and squeakings might easily be construed into thumps, bumps, and blood-curdling groans. The girls would often get up scares among themselves and be absolutely convinced that a tragedy, either real or supernatural, was being enacted behind the oak door.

Miss Birks, sensible and matter-of-fact as became a headmistress, laughed at her pupils' notions, and declared that her chief objection to the peculiar clause in her lease was the waste of a good bedroom which would have been invaluable as an extra dormitory. She hung a thick plush curtain over the doorway, and utterly tabooed the subject of the mystery. She could not, however, prevent the girls talking about it among themselves, and to them the barred room became a veritable Bluebeard's chamber. At night they scuttled past it with averted gaze and fingers stuffed in their ears, having an uneasy apprehension lest a skeleton hand should suddenly draw aside the curtain and a face—be it ghost or grinning goblin—peer at them out of the darkness. They would dare each other to stand and listen, or to pass the door alone, and among the younger ones a character for heroism stood or fell on the capacity of venturing nearest to the so-called "bogey hole".

Though Miss Birks might well regret such a disability in her lease of the Dower House, she was proud of the old-world aspect of the place, and treasured up any traditions of the past that she could gather together. She had carefully written down all surviving details of the Franciscan convent, having after endless trouble secured some account of it from rare books and manuscripts in the possession of some of the country gentry in the neighbourhood. Beyond the dates of its founding and dissolution, and the names of its abbesses, there was little to be learnt, though a few old records of business transactions gave an idea of its extent and importance.

Dearly as she valued the fourteenth-century origin of her establishment, Miss Birks did not sacrifice comfort to any love of the antique. Inside the ancient walls everything was strictly modern and hygienic, with the latest patterns of desks, the most sanitary wall-papers, and each up-to-date appliance that educational authorities might suggest or devise. Could the Grey Nuns have but returned and taken a peep into the well-equipped little chemical laboratory, they would probably have fancied themselves in the chamber of a wizard in league with the fiends of darkness, and have crossed themselves in pious fear at the sight of the bottles and retorts; the nicely-fitted gymnasium would have puzzled them sorely; and a hockey match have aroused their sincerest horror. *Tempora mutantur, nos et mutamur in illis*—"the times are changed, and we are changed with them!" Though we have lost something of the picturesqueness of mediaeval life, the childlike faith of a childlike age, the simplicity of a nation only groping to feel its strength, we have surely gained in the long years of growth, in the gradual awakening to the thousand things undreamt of by our forefathers, and can justly deem that our lasses have inherited a golden harvest of thought and experience from those who have trod before them the thorny and difficult pathway that leads to knowledge.

Such were the picturesque and highly-appreciated surroundings at the Dower House, and now a word on that much more important subject, the girls themselves.

Miss Birks only received twenty pupils, all over fourteen years of age, therefore there was no division into upper and lower school. Five elder girls constituted the Sixth, and the rest were placed according to their capabilities in two sections of the Fifth Form. Of these V<small>B</small> was considerably the larger, and containing, as it did, the younger, cruder, and more-boisterous spirits, was, in the opinion of the mistresses, the portion which required the finer tact and the greater amount of careful management. It was not that its members gave any special trouble, but they were somewhat in the position of novices, not yet thoroughly versed in the traditions of the little community, and needing skill and patience during the process of their initiation. Almost insensibly the nine seemed to split up into separate parties. Romola Harvey, Barbara Marshall, and Elyned Hughes lived in the same town, and knew each other at home; a sufficient bond of union to knit them in a close friendship which they were unwilling to share with anybody else. The news from Springfield, their native place, formed their chief subject of interest, and those who could not understand or discuss it must necessarily be in the position of outsiders. Evie Bennett, Annie Pridwell, and Betty Scott were lively, high-spirited girls, so full of irrepressible fun that they were apt to drop the deeper element out of life altogether. It was difficult ever to find them in a serious mood, their jokes were incessant, and they certainly well earned the nickname of "the three gigglers" which was generally bestowed upon them.

Until Christmas, Deirdre Sullivan and Dulcie Wilcox had rejoiced in the possession of a bedroom to themselves, a circumstance which had allowed them the opportunity of cultivating their friendship till they had become the most exclusive chums in the whole of the school. Deirdre, the elder by six months, was a picturesque, rather interesting-looking girl, with beautiful, expressive grey eyes, a delicate colour, and a neat, slim little figure. Dulcie, on the contrary, much to her mortification, was inclined to stoutness. She resembled a painting by Rubens, for her plump cheeks were pink as carnations, and her ruddy hair was of that warm shade of Venetian red so beloved by the old masters. It was a sore point with poor Dulcie that, however badly her head ached, or however limp or indisposed she might feel, her high colour never faded, and no pathetic hollows ever appeared in her cheeks.

"I get no sympathy when I'm ill," she confided to Deirdre. "On that day when I turned faint in the algebra class, Miss Harding had said only an hour before: 'You do look well, child!' I wish I were as pale and thin as Elyned Hughes, then I might get petted and excused lessons. As it is, no one believes me when I complain."

Dulcie, who possessed an intense admiration for her chum, struggled perpetually to mould herself on Deirdre's model, sometimes with rather comical results. Deirdre's romantic tendencies caused her to affect the particular style of the heroine of nearly every fresh book she read, and she changed continually from an air of reserved and stately dignity to one of sparkling vivacity, according to her latest favourite in fiction. With

Deirdre it was an easy matter enough to assume a manner; but Dulcie, who merely copied her friend slavishly, often aroused mirth in the schoolroom by her extraordinary poses.

"Who is it now, Dulcie?" the girls would ask. "Rebecca of York, or the Scarlet Pimpernel? You might drop us a hint, so that we could tell, and treat you accordingly."

And Dulcie, being an unimaginative and really rather obtuse little person, though she knew she was being laughed at, could never quite fathom the reason why, and continued to lisp or drawl, or to attempt to look dignified, or to sparkle, with a praiseworthy perseverance worthy of a better object.

CHAPTER III

A Mysterious Schoolfellow

It is all very well for a girl to be shy on her first night at school. A certain amount of embarrassment is indeed considered almost "good form" in a new-comer, indicative of her realization of the privileges which she is about to enjoy, and the comparative unworthiness of any previous establishment she may have attended. But when her uncommunicative attitude is unduly prolonged, what was at first labelled mere becoming bashfulness is termed stupidity, closeness, stuck-up conceit, or intentional rudeness by her companions, who highly resent any repulse of their offers of friendship. Gerda Thorwaldson, after nearly a fortnight at the Dower House, seemed as much a stranger as on the evening when she arrived. She was neither uncivil nor disobliging, but no efforts on the part of her schoolmates were able to penetrate the thick barrier of her reserve. She appeared most unwilling to enter into any particulars of her former life, and beyond the fact that she had been educated chiefly in Germany no information could be dragged from her.

"You've only to hint at her home, and she shuts up like an oyster," said Annie Pridwell aggrievedly. Annie had a natural love of biography. She delighted in hearing her comrades' experiences, and was so well up in everybody's private affairs that she could have written a "Who's Who" of the school.

"You ought to know, Deirdre," she continued. "Doesn't she tell you anything at all in your bedroom?"

"Hardly opens her mouth," replied Deirdre. "You wouldn't believe how difficult it is to talk to her. She just says 'Yes' or 'No', and occasionally asks a question, but she certainly tells us nothing about herself."

"Never met with anyone so mum in my life," added Dulcie.

The question of Gerda's nationality still weighed upon Dulcie's spirits. In her opinion a girl who could speak a foreign language with such absolute fluency did not deserve to be called English, and she was further disturbed by a hint which got abroad that the new girl had been requisitioned to the school for the particular purpose of talking German.

"If that's so, why has she been poked upon us?" she demanded indignantly. "Why wasn't she put in a dormitory with somebody who'd appreciate her better?—Marcia Richards, for instance, who says she 'envies our advantages'."

"Ask Miss Birks!"

"Oh, I dare say! But I don't like people who listen to everything and say nothing. It gives one the idea they mean to sneak some day."

Though Gerda's attitude regarding her own affairs was uncommunicative, she nevertheless appeared to take a profound interest in her present surroundings. As Dulcie had noticed, she listened to everything, and no detail, however small, seemed to escape her. She was anxious to learn all she could concerning the old house, the neighbourhood, and the families who resided near, and would ask an occasional question on the subject, often blushing scarlet as she put her queries.

"Why, I should think you could draw a plan of the house!" said Dulcie one day. "What does it matter whether the larder is underneath our dormitory or not? You can't dive through the floor and purloin tarts!"

"No, of course not. I was only wondering," replied Gerda, shrinking into her shell again.

Nevertheless, later on in the afternoon, Dulcie suddenly came across her measuring the landing with a yard tape.

"What in the name of all that's wonderful are you doing?" exclaimed the much-surprised damsel.

"Oh, nothing, nothing!" said Gerda, hastily rolling up her tape measure, and slipping it into her pocket. "Only just an idea that came into my head. I wanted to know the length of the passage, that was all!"

"What a most extraordinary thing to want to know! Really, Gerda, you're the queerest girl I ever met. Is it having lived in Germany that makes you so odd?"

"I suppose it must be," murmured Gerda, escaping as rapidly as possible into the schoolroom.

I have said before that owing to the unique situation of the Dower House the girls were allowed an amount of liberty in their play-hours which could not so easily have been granted to them at other schools. They wandered freely about the headland without a mistress, and so far had never abused their privileges, either by getting into danger or staying out beyond the specified time.

Though as a rule they rambled in trios, on the first of February the whole of Form V$_B$ might have been seen walking together over the warren. They had a motive for their excursion, for it was St. Perran's Day, and St. Perran was the patron saint of the district. At the end of the promontory there was a small spring dedicated to his memory, and according to ancient legends, anybody who on his anniversary dropped a pin into this well might learn her luck for the coming year. Formerly all the lads and lasses from the villages of Pontperran, Porthmorvan, and Perranwrack used to come to deck the well and try their fortunes, but their annual visitation having degenerated into a rather riotous and undesirable ceremony, Mrs. Trevellyan had put up extra trespass notices, and given strict orders to her gamekeeper to exclude the public from the headland.

Knowing of the ancient custom which had been practised from time immemorial, it was of course only in schoolgirl nature to want to test the powers of divination attributed to the old well. The Sixth Form, who considered themselves almost grown up, treated the affair with ridicule, and the members of V$_A$, who copied their seniors slavishly, likewise affected a supreme contempt for so childish a proceeding; but V$_B$, being still at an age when superstition holds an immense attraction, trotted off *en bloc* to pay their respects to St. Perran. Each, in deference to the long-established tradition of the neighbourhood, bore a garland of ferns and other greeneries, and each came armed with the necessary pin that was to work the spell.

"Jessie Macpherson says we're a set of sillies," volunteered Betty Scott. "But I don't care—I wouldn't miss St. Perran's Day for anything."

"My wish came true last year," put in Barbara Marshall.

"Oh, I do hope I shall have some luck!" shivered Elyned Hughes.

The well in question lay in a slight hollow, a kind of narrow gully, where in wet weather a small stream ambled between the rocks and ran down to the sea. In the mild Cornish climate ferns were growing here fresh and green, ignoring the presence of winter; and dog's-mercury, strawberry-leaved cinquefoil, and other early plants were pushing up strong leaves in preparation for the springtime. The famous well was nothing but a shallow basin of rock, into which the little stream flowed leisurely, and, having partially filled it, trickled away through a gap, and became for a yard or two merged in a patch of swampy herbage. Overhung with long fronds of lady-fern and tufts of hawkweed, it had a picturesque aspect, and the water seemed to gurgle slowly and mysteriously, as if it were trying in some unknown language to reveal a secret.

The girls clustered round, and began in orthodox fashion to hang their garlands on the leafless branches of a stunted tree that stretched itself over the spring. They were in various moods, some giggling, some half-awed, some silent, and some chattering.

"It isn't as high as it was last year, so I don't believe it will work so well," said Evie Bennett. "St. Perran must be in a bad temper, and hasn't looked after it properly. Tiresome old man, why can't he remember his own day?"

"He's got to do double duty, poor old chap!" laughed Betty Scott. "You forget he's the patron saint of the sailors as well, and is supposed to be out at sea attracting the fish. Perhaps he just hadn't time this morning, and thought the well would do."

"Let well alone, in fact," giggled Evie.

"Oh, shut her up for her bad pun! Dip her head in the water! Make her try her luck first!"

"Pleased to accommodate you, I'm sure. Here's my pin," returned Evie. "Now, if you're ready, I'll begin and consult the oracle."

St. Perran's ceremony had to be performed in due order, or it was supposed to be of no effect. First of all, Evie solemnly dropped her pin in the well, as a species of votive offering, while silently she murmured a wish. Then placing a small piece of stick on the surface of the water in the exact centre of the basin, she repeated the time-honoured formula:

"Perran, Perran of the well,What I've wished I may not tell,'Tis but known to me and you,Help me then to bring it true".

All eyes were fixed eagerly on the piece of stick, which was already commencing to circle round in the water. If it found its way successfully through the gap, and was washed down by the stream, it was a sign that St. Perran had it safely and would attend to the matter; but if it were stranded on the edge of the basin, the wish would remain unfulfilled. Round and round went the tiny twig, bobbing and dancing in the eddies; but, alas! the water was low this February, and instead of sweeping the twig triumphantly through the aperture, it only washed it to one side, and left it clinging to some overhanging fronds of fern that dipped into the spring. Evie heaved a tragic sigh of disappointment.

"I'm done for at any rate!" she groaned. "St. Perran won't have anything to say to me this year. Oh, and it was such a lovely wish! I'll tell you what it was, now it's not going to come off. I wished some aviator would ask me to have a seat in his aeroplane, and take me right over to America in it!"

The girls tittered.

"What a particularly likely wish to be fulfilled! No, my hearty, you can't expect St. Perran to have anything to do with aeroplanes," said Betty Scott. "The good old saint probably abhors all modern inventions. I'm going to wish for something easy and probable."

"What?"

"Ah! wouldn't you like to know? I shan't tell you, even if I fail. Shall I try next?"

Whatever Betty's easy and probable desire may have been, the result was bad, and her stick, after several thrilling gyrations, tagged itself on to Evie's under the cluster of fern. She bore her ill luck like a stoic.

"One can't have everything in this world," she philosophized. "Perhaps I'll get it next year instead. Deirdre Sullivan, you deserve to lose your own for sniggering! This trial ought to be taken solemnly. We'll get St. Perran's temper up if we make fun of it."

"I thought he was out at sea, attracting the fishes!" said Deirdre.

"I'm not sure that Cornish saints can't be in two places at once, just to show their superiority over Devonshire ones. Well, go on! Laugh if you like! But don't expect St. Perran to take any interest in you!"

It certainly seemed as though the patron of the well had for once forsaken his favourite haunt. Girl after girl wished her wish and repeated her spell, but invariably to meet with the same ill fortune, till a melancholy little clump of eight sticks testified to the general failure.

"Have we all lost? No, Gerda Thorwaldson hasn't tried! Where's Gerda? She's got to do the same as anybody else! Gerda Thorwaldson, where are you?"

Gerda for the moment had been missing, but at the sound of her name she scrambled down from the rocks above the well, looking rather red and conscious.

"What were you doing up there?" asked Dulcie sharply. "It's your turn to try the omen. Go along, quick; we shall have to be jogging back in half a jiff."

Gerda paused for a moment, and with face full towards the sea muttered her wish with moving lips; then turning to the tree, she carefully counted the third bough from the bottom, and the third twig on the bough. Breaking off her due portion, she twisted it round three times, and holding it between the third fingers of either hand, dropped it into the water, while she rapidly repeated the magic formula:

"Perran, Perran of the well,What I've wished I may not tell,'Tis but known to me and you,Help me then to bring it true".

The girls watched rather half-heartedly. They were growing a little tired of the performance. They fully expected the ninth stick to drift the same way as its predecessors, but to everybody's astonishment it made one rapid circle of the basin, and bobbed successfully through the gap.

"It's gone! it's gone!" cried Betty Scott in wild excitement. "St. Perran's working after all. Oh, why didn't he do it for me?"

"How funny it should be the only one!" said Elyned Hughes.

"I believe the water's running faster than it did before," commented Romola Harvey. "Has the old saint turned on the tap?"

"Shall I get my wish?" said Gerda, who stood by with shining eyes.

"Of course you'll get it—certain sure. And jolly fortunate you are too. You've won the luck of the whole Form. Don't I wish I were you, just!"

"You're evidently St. Perran's favourite!" laughed Annie Pridwell.

"Come along, it's nearly time for call-over. We'll be late if we don't sprint," said Barbara Marshall, consulting her watch, and starting at a run on the path that led back to the Dower House.

"It was a funny thing that our sticks should all 'stick', and Gerda's just sail off as easily as you like," said Deirdre that evening, as, with Dulcie, she gave an account of the occurrence to Phyllis Rowland, a member of the Sixth. As one of the elect of the school, Phyllis would not have condescended to consult the famous oracle, but she nevertheless took a sneaking interest in the annual ceremony, and was anxious to know how St. Perran's votaries had fared.

"Did you do it really properly?" she enquired. "An old woman at Perranwrack once told me it wasn't any use at all if you forgot the least thing."

"Why, we hung up our garlands and then wished, and said the rhyme, and threw in our sticks."

"Oh, that isn't half enough. Where were you looking when you wished? Facing the sea? Your stick should be chosen from the third twig on the third branch, and it ought to be turned round three times, and held between your third fingers. Did you do all that?"

The faces of Deirdre and Dulcie were a study.

"No, we didn't. But Gerda Thorwaldson did it—every bit. And the water came down ever so much faster for her turn, too."

"Probably she went behind the well, and cleared the channel of the stream. That's a well-known dodge to make the water flow quicker, and help the saint to work."

"I certainly saw her climbing down the rocks," gasped Dulcie.

"Then she's a cleverer girl than I took her for, and deserves her luck," laughed Phyllis. "Look here, I can't stay wasting time any longer. I've got my prep to do. Ta, ta! Don't let St. Perran blight your young lives. Try him again next year."

Left alone, Deirdre and Dulcie subsided simultaneously on to a bench.

"It beats me altogether," said Dulcie, shaking her head. "How did she manage to do it? How did she know? Who told her?"

"That's the puzzler," returned Deirdre. "Certainly not Phyllis, and I don't believe anybody else ever heard of those extra dodges. Gerda's only been a fortnight at the school, and says she's never been in Cornwall in her life before, so how could she know? Yet she did it all so pat."

"It's queer, to say the least of it."

"Do you know, Dulcie, I think there's something mysterious about Gerda. I've noticed it ever since she came. She seems all the time to be trying to hide something. She won't tell us a scrap about herself, and yet she's always asking questions."

"What's she up to then?"

"That's what I want to find out. It's evidently something she doesn't want people to know. She ought to be watched. I vote we keep an eye on her."

"I really believe we ought to."

"But mind, you mustn't let her suspect we notice anything. That would give the show away at once. Lie low's our motto."

"Right you are!" agreed Dulcie. "Mum's the word!"

CHAPTER IV

"The King of the Castle"

The members of VB often congratulated themselves that their special classroom was decidedly larger than that of the Sixth or of VA. They were apt to boast of their superior accommodation, and would never admit the return argument that being so much larger a form, their room really allowed less space per girl, and was therefore actually inferior to its rivals. On one February evening the whole nine were sitting round the fire, luxuriating in half an hour's delicious idleness before the bell rang for "second prep.". Those who had been first in the field had secured the basket-chairs, but the majority squatted on the hearth-rug, making as close a ring as they could, for the night was cold, and there was a nip of frost in the air.

"Now, don't anybody begin to talk sense, please!" pleaded Betty Scott, leaning a golden-brown head mock-sentimentally on Annie Pridwell's shoulder. "My poor little brains are just about pumped out with maths., and what's left of them will be wanted for French prep. later on. This is the silly season, so I hope no one will endeavour to improve my mind."

"They'd have a Herculean task before them if they did!" sniggered Annie. "Betty, your head may be empty, but it's jolly heavy, all the same. I wish you'd kindly remove it from my shoulder."

"You mass of ingratitude! It was a mark of supreme affection—a kind of 'They grew in beauty side by side', don't you know!"

"I don't want to know. Not if it involves nursing your weight. Oh, yes! go to Barbara, by all means, if she'll have you. I'm not in the least offended."

"That big basket-chair oughtn't to be monopolized by one," asserted Evie Bennett. "It's quite big enough for two. Here, Deirdre, make room for me. Don't be stingy, you must give me another inch. That's better. It's rather a squash, but we can just manage."

"You're cuckooing me out!" protested Deirdre.

"No, no, I'm not. There's space for two in this nest. We're a pair of doves:

"'Coo,' said the turtle dove,'Coo,' said she".

"I'll say something more to the point, if you don't take care. What a lot of sillies you are!"

"Then please deign to enlarge our intellects. We're hanging upon your words. Betty can stop her ears, if she thinks it will be too great a strain on her slender brains. What is it to be? A recitation from Milton, or a dissertation on the evils of levity? Miss Sullivan, your audience awaits you. Mr. Chairman, will you please introduce the lecturer?"

"Ladies and gentlemen, I hasten to explain that owing to severe indisposition I am unable to be present to-night," returned Deirdre promptly.

"Oh, Irish of the Irish!" laughed the girls. "Did you say it on purpose, or did it come unconsciously?"

"I wish I were Irish. Somehow I never say funny things, not even if I try," lamented Dulcie.

"Because you couldn't. You're a dear fat dumpling, and dumplings never are funny, you know—it's against nature."

"It's not my fault if I'm fat," said Dulcie plaintively. "People say 'Laugh and grow fat', so why shouldn't a plump person be funny?"

"They are funny—very funny—though not quite in the way you mean."

"Oh, look here! Don't be horrid!"

"You began it yourself."

"Children, don't barge!" interrupted Romola Harvey. "You really are rather a set of lunatics to-night. Can't anyone tell a story?"

"I was taught to call fibbing a sin in the days of my youth," retorted Betty Scott, assuming a serious countenance.

"You—you ragtimer! I mean a real story—a tale—a legend—a romance —or whatever you choose to call it."

"Don't know any."

"We've used them all up," said Evie Bennett, yawning lustily. "We all know the legend of the Abbess Gertrude—it's Miss Birks's favourite chestnut—and what she said to the Commissioner who came to confiscate the convent: and we've had the one about Monmouth's rebellion till it's as stale as stale can be. I defy anybody to have the hardihood to repeat it."

"Aren't there any other tales about the neighbourhood?" asked Gerda Thorwaldson. It was the first remark that she had made.

"Oh, I don't think so. The old castle's very sparse in legends. I suppose there ought to be a few, but they're mostly forgotten."

"Who used to live there?"

"Trevellyans. There always have been Trevellyans—hosts of them—though now there's nobody left but Mrs. Trevellyan and Ronnie."

"Who's Ronnie?"

More than half a dozen answers came instantly.

"Ronnie? Why, he's just Ronnie."

"Mrs. Trevellyan's great-nephew."

"The dearest darling!"

"You never saw anyone so sweet."

"We all of us adore him."

"We call him 'The King of the Castle'."

"They've been away, staying in London."

"But they're coming back this week."

"Is he grown up?" enquired Gerda casually.

"Grown up!" exploded the girls. "He's not quite six!"

"He lives with Mrs. Trevellyan," explained Betty, "because he hasn't got any father or mother of his own."

"Oh, Betty, he has!" burst out Barbara.

"Well, that's the first I ever heard of them, then. I thought he was an orphan."

"He's as good as an orphan, poor little chap."

"Why?"

"Nobody ever mentions his father."

"Why on earth not?"

"Oh, I don't know! There's something mysterious. Mrs. Trevellyan doesn't like it talked about. Nobody dare even drop a hint to her."

"What's wrong with Ronnie's father?"

"I tell you I don't know, except that I believe he did something he shouldn't have."

"Rough on Ronnie."

"Ronnie doesn't know, of course, and nobody would be cruel enough to tell him. You must promise you'll none of you mention what I've said. Not to anybody."

"Rather not! You can trust us!" replied all.

It was perhaps only natural that the affairs of the Castle should seem important to the dwellers at the Dower House. The two buildings lay so near together, yet were so isolated in their position as regarded other habitations, that they united in many ways for their mutual convenience. If Miss Birks's gardener was going to the town he would execute commissions for the Castle, as well as for his own mistress; and, on the other hand, the Castle chauffeur would call at the Dower House for letters to be sent by the late post. Mrs. Trevellyan was a widow with no family of her own. She had adopted her great-nephew Ronald while he was still quite a baby, and he could remember no other home than hers. The little fellow was the one delight and solace of her advancing years.

Her life centred round Ronnie; she thought continually of his interests, and made many plans for his future. He was her constant companion, and his pretty, affectionate ways and merry chatter did much to help her to forget old griefs. He was a most winning, engaging child, a favourite with everybody, and reigned undoubtedly as monarch in the hearts of all who had the care of him. It was partly on Ronnie's account, and partly because she really loved young people, that Mrs. Trevellyan took so much notice of the pupils at the Dower House. On her nephew's behalf she would have preferred a boys' preparatory school for neighbour, but even girls over fourteen were better than nobody; they made an element of youth that was good for Ronnie, and prevented the Castle from seeming too dull. The knowledge that he might perhaps meet his friends on the headland gave an object to the little boy's daily walk, and the jokes and banter with which they generally greeted him provided him with a subject for conversation afterwards.

The girls on their part showed the liveliest interest in anything connected with the Castle. They would watch the motor passing in and out of the great gates, would peep from their top windows to look at the gardeners mowing the lawns, and would even count the rooks' nests that were built in the grove of elm trees. Occasionally Mrs. Trevellyan would ask the whole school to tea, and that was regarded as so immense a treat that the girls always looked forward to the delightful chance that some fortunate morning an invitation might be forthcoming.

Mrs. Trevellyan had been staying in London at the beginning of the term, but early in February she returned home again. On the day after her arrival the girls were walking back from a hockey practice on the warren, swinging their way along the narrow tracks between last year's bracken and heather, or having an impromptu long-jump contest where a small stream crossed the path.

"It's so jolly to see the flag up again at the Castle," said Evie Bennett, looking at the turret where the Union Jack was flying bravely in the breeze. "I always feel as if it's a kind of national defence. Any ships sailing by would know it was England they were passing."

"I like it because it means Mrs. Trevellyan's at home," said Deirdre Sullivan. "A place seems so forlorn when the family's away. Did Ronnie come back too, last night?"

"Yes, Hilda Marriott saw him from the window this morning. He was going down the road with his new governess. Why, there he is—actually watching for us, the darling!"

The girls had to pass close to a turnstile that led from the Castle grounds into the warren, and here, perched astride the top rail of the gate, evidently on the look-out for them, a small boy was waving his cap in frantic welcome. He was a pretty little fellow, with the bluest of eyes and the fairest of skins, and the lightest of flaxen hair, and he seemed dimpling all over his merry face with delight at the meeting. The girls simply made a rush for him, and he was handed about from one to another, struggling in laughing protest, till at last he wriggled himself free, and retiring behind the turnstile, held the gate as a barrier.

"I knew you'd be coming past, so I got leave to play here. Thank you all for your Christmas cards," he said gaily. "Yes—I like my new governess. Her name's Miss Herbert, and she's ripping. Auntie's going to ask you to tea. I want to show you my engine I got at Christmas. It goes round the floor and it really puffs. You'll come?"

"Oh! we'll come all right," chuckled the girls. "We've got something at the Dower House to show you, too. No, we shan't tell you what it is—it's to be a surprise. Oh, goody! There's the bell! Ta-ta! We must be off! If we don't fly, we shall all be late for call-over. No, you're not to come through the gate to say good-bye! Go back, you rascal! You know you're not allowed on the warren!"

As the big bell at the Dower House was clang-clanging its loudest, the girls set off at a run. There was not a minute to be lost if they meant to be in their places to answer "Present" to their names; and missing the roll-call meant awkward explanations with Miss Birks. One only, oblivious of the urgency of the occasion, lingered behind. Gerda Thorwaldson had stood apart while the others greeted Ronnie, merely looking on as if the meeting were of no interest to her. Nobody had taken the slightest notice of her, or had indeed remembered her existence at the moment. She counted for so little with her schoolfellows that it never struck them to introduce her to their favourite; in fact they had been totally occupied among themselves in fighting for possession of him. She remained now, until the very last school sports' cap was round the corner and out of sight. Then she dashed through the turnstile, and overtaking Ronnie, thrust a packet of chocolates, rather awkwardly, into his hand.

The bell had long ceased clanging, and Miss Birks had closed the call-over book when Gerda entered the schoolroom. As she would offer no explanation of her lateness, she was given a page of French poetry to learn, to teach her next time to regard punctuality as a cardinal virtue. She took her punishment with absolute stolidity.

"What a queer girl she is! She never seems to care what happens," said Dulcie. "I should mind if Miss Birks glared at me in that way, to say nothing of a whole page of *Athalie*."

"She looked as if she'd been crying when she came in," remarked Deirdre.

"She's not crying now, at any rate. She simply looks unapproachable. What made her so late? She was with us on the warren."

"How should I know? If she won't tell, she won't. You might as well try to make a mule gallop uphill as attempt to get even the slightest, most ordinary, everyday scrap of information out of such a sphinx as Gerda Thorwaldson."

CHAPTER V

Practical Geography

MISS BIRKS often congratulated herself on the fact that the smallness of her school allowed her to give a proportionately large amount of individual attention to her pupils. There was no possibility at the Dower House for even the laziest girl to shirk lessons and shield her ignorance behind the general bulk of information possessed by the Form. Backward girls, dull girls, delicate girls—all had their special claims considered and their fair chances accorded. There was no question of "passing in a crowd". Each pupil stood or fell on the merits of her own work, and every item of her progress was noted with as much care as if she were the sole charge of the establishment. Miss Birks had many theories of education, some gleaned from national conferences of teachers, and others of her own evolving, all on the latest of modern lines. One of her pet theories was the practical application, whenever possible, of every lesson learnt. According to the season the girls botanized, geologized, collected caterpillars and chrysalides, or hunted for marine specimens on the shore, vying with each other in a friendly rivalry as to which could secure the best contributions for the school museum.

There was no subject, however, in Miss Birks's estimation which led itself more readily to practical illustration than geography. Every variety of physical feature was examined in the original situation, so that watersheds, tributaries, table-lands, currents, and comparative elevations became solid facts instead of mere book statements, and each girl was taught to make her own map of the district.

"I believe we've examined everything except an iceberg and a volcano," declared Betty Scott one day, "and I verily believe Miss Birks is on the look-out for both—hoped an iceberg might be washed ashore during those few cold days we had in January, and you know she told us Beacon Hill was the remains of an extinct volcano. I expect she wished it might burst out suddenly again, like Vesuvius, just to show us how it did it!"

"Wouldn't we squeal and run if we heard rumblings and saw jets of steam coming up?" commented Evie Bennett. "I don't think many of us would stay to do scientific work, and take specimens of the lava."

"Where are we going this afternoon?" asked Elyned Hughes.

"Mapping, Miss Birks said. We're to make for the old windmill, and then draw a radius of six miles, from Kergoff to Avonporth. Hurry up, you others! It's after two, and Miss Harding's waiting on the terrace. What a set of slow-coaches you are!"

It was the turn of VB to have a practical geography demonstration, and they started, therefore, under the guidance of the second mistress, to survey the physical features of a certain portion of the neighbourhood, and record them in a map. Each girl was furnished by Miss Birks with a paper of questions, intended to be a guide to her observations:

1.—Using the windmill as a centre, what direction do the roads take?

2.—What villages or farms must be noted?

3.—What rivers or streams, and their courses?

4.—What lakes or ponds?

5.—The general outline of the coast?

6.—Are there hills or mountains?

7.—What historical monuments should be marked with a cross?

Armed with their instructions, pocket compasses, and note-books, the girls set off in cheerful spirits. They dearly loved these country rambles, and heartily approved of this particular method of education. It was a beautiful bright afternoon towards the middle of February, one of those glorious days that seem to anticipate the spring, and to make one forget that winter exists at all. The sky was cloudless and blue, not with the serene blue of summer, but with that fainter, almost greenish shade so noticeable in the early months of the year, and growing pearly-white where it touched the horizon. There was a joyous feeling of returning life in the air; a thrush, perhaps remembering that it was St. Valentine's Eve, carolled with full rich voice in the bare thorn tree, small birds chased each other among the bushes, and great flocks of rooks were feeding up and down the ploughed fields. In sheltered corners an early wild flower or two had forestalled the season, and the girls picked an occasional celandine star or primrose bud, and even a few cherished violets. The catkins on the hazels were shaking down showers of golden pollen, and the sallows were covered with silky, silvery tufts of palm; the low sycamores in the hedge showed rosy buds almost ready to burst, and shoots of bramble or sprays of newly-opened honeysuckle leaves formed green patches here and there on the old walls.

The girls walked at a brisk, swinging pace, in no particular order, so long as they kept together, and with licence to stop to examine specimens within reasonable limits of time. Miss Harding, who was herself a fairly good naturalist, might be consulted at any moment, and all unknown or doubtful objects, if portable, were popped in a basket and taken back to be identified by the supreme authority, Miss Birks.

Though they fully appreciated the warren as a playground, it was delightful to have a wider field for their activities, and the opportunity of making some fresh find or some interesting discovery to report at headquarters. Miss Birks kept a Nature Diary hung on the wall of the big schoolroom, and there was keen competition as to which should be the first to supply the various items that made up its weekly chronicle. It was even on record that Rhoda Wilkins once ran a whole mile at top speed in order to steal a march on Emily Northwood, and claim for VA the proud honour of announcing the first bird's nest of the year.

The special point for which the girls were bound this afternoon was a ruined windmill that stood on a small eminence, and formed rather a landmark in the district. From here an excellent view might be obtained of both the outline of the coast and the course of the little river that ambled down from the hills and poured itself into the sea by the tiny village of Kergoff. No fitter spot could have been chosen for a general survey, and as the girls reached the platform on which the building stood, and ranged themselves under its picturesque ragged sails, they pulled out their note-books and got to business.

It was a glorious panorama that lay below them—brown heathery common and rugged cliff, steep crags against which the growing tide was softly lapping, a babbling little river that wound a noisy course between boulders and over rounded, age-worn stones, tumbling in leaps from the hills, dancing through the meadows, and flowing with a strong, steady swirl through the whitewashed hamlet ere it widened out to join the harbour. And beyond all there was the sea—the shimmering, glittering sea—rolling quietly in with slow, heavy swell, and dashing with a dull boom against the lighthouse rocks, bearing far off on its bosom a chance vessel southward bound, and floating one by one the little craft that had been beached in the anchorage, till they strained at their cables, and bobbed gaily on the rising water. Only one or two of the girls perhaps realized the intense beauty and poetry of the scene; most were busy noting the natural features, and calculating possible distances, marking here a farm or there a hill crest, and trying to reproduce in some creditable fashion the eccentric windings of the river.

"That little crag below us just blocks the view of the road," said Deirdre. "I can't get the bend in at all. Do you mind, Miss Harding, if some of us go to the bottom of the hill and trace it out?"

"Certainly, if you like," replied the mistress. "I'm tired, so I shall wait for you here. It won't take you longer than ten minutes."

"Oh, dear, no! We'll race down. I say, who'll come?"

Dulcie, Betty, Annie, Barbara, and Gerda were among the energetically disposed, but Evie, Romola, and Elyned preferred to wait with Miss Harding.

"We'll copy yours when you come back," they announced shamelessly.

"Oh, we'll see about that! Ta-ta!" cried the others, as they started at a fair pace down the hill.

The road was certainly the most winding of any they had attempted to trace that afternoon. It twisted like a cork-screw between high banks, then hiding beneath a steep crag plunged suddenly through a small fir wood, and crossed the river by a stone bridge. The girls had descended at a jog trot, trying to take their bearings as they went. Owing to the great height of the banks it was impossible to see what was below, therefore it was only when they had passed the wood that they noticed for the first time an old grey house on the farther side of the bridge. It was built so close to the stream that its long veranda actually overhung the water, which swept swirling against the lower wall of the building. Many years must have passed since it last held a tenant, for creepers stretched long tendrils over the broken windows, and grass grew green in the gutters. The dilapidated gate, the weed-grown garden, the weather-worn, paintless woodwork, the damp-stained walls, the damaged roof, all gave it an air of almost indescribable melancholy, so utterly abandoned, deserted, and entirely neglected did it appear.

"Hallo! Why, this must be 'Forster's Folly'!" exclaimed Barbara. "I'd no idea we were so close to it. We couldn't see even the chimneys from the windmill."

"What an extraordinary name for an even more extraordinary house!" said Deirdre. "Who in the name of all that's weird was 'Forster'? And why is this rat's-hall-looking place called his folly?"

"He was a lawyer in the neighbourhood, I believe, and, like some lawyers, just a little bit too sharp. It was when the railway was going to be made. He heard it was coming this way, and he calculated it would just have to cut across this piece of land, so he bought the field and built this house on it in a tremendous hurry, because he thought he could claim big compensation from the railway company; and then after all they took the line round by Avonporth instead, five miles away, and didn't want to buy his precious house, so he'd had all the trouble and expense for nothing."

"Served him right!" grunted the girls.

"They say he was furious," continued Barbara. "He was so disgusted that he never even painted the woodwork or laid out the garden properly. He tried to let it, but nobody wanted it; so he was obliged to come and live in it himself for economy's sake. He was an old bachelor, and he and a sour old housekeeper were here for a year or two, and then he died very suddenly, and rather mysteriously. His relations came and took away the furniture, but they haven't been able to sell the house, it's in such a queer, out-of-the-way place. Then everybody in the neighbourhood said it was haunted, and not a soul would go near it for love or money."

"It looks haunted," said Dulcie with a shiver. "Just the kind of lonely-moated-grange place where you'd expect to see a 'woman in white' at the window."

"Never saw anything so spooky in my life before," agreed Deirdre.

"Did you say it used to belong to Mr. Forster, the lawyer?" asked Gerda. "The one who had business at St. Gonstan?"

"I don't know where he had business, but it was certainly Mr. Forster, the lawyer. I don't suppose there'd be more than one."

"When did he die?"

"About five years ago, I fancy. Why do you want to know?"

"Oh, nothing! It doesn't matter in the least," returned Gerda, shrinking into her shell again.

"It's the weirdest, queerest place I've ever seen," said Deirdre. "Do let's go a little nearer. Ugh! What would you take to spend a night here alone?"

"Nothing in the wide world you could offer me," protested Betty.

"I'd go stark, staring mad!" affirmed Annie.

"Hallo!" squealed Dulcie suddenly. "What's become of Gerda? She's sneaked off!"

"Why, there she is, peeping through one of the broken windows!"

"Oh, I say! I must have a squint too, to see if there's really a ghost!" fluttered Annie.

"You goose! You wouldn't see ghosts by daylight!"

"Well, I don't care anyhow. I'm going to peep. Cuckoo, Gerda! What can you see inside?"

When Annie Pridwell led the way, it followed of necessity that the others went after her, so they scurried to catch her up, and all ran in a body over the bridge and into the nettle-grown garden. Gerda was still perched on the window-sill of one of the lower rooms, and she turned to her schoolfellows with a strange light in her eyes and a look of unwonted excitement on her face.

"I put my hand through the broken pane and pulled back the catch," she volunteered. "We've only to push the window up and we could go inside."

"Oh! Dare we?"

"Suppose the ghost caught us?"

"Oh, I say! Do let us go!"

"It would be such gorgeous sport!"

"I'm game, if you all are."

As usual it was Annie Pridwell who led the adventure. Pushing up the window, she climbed over the sill and dropped inside, then turning round offered a hand to Gerda, who sprang eagerly after her. It was imperative for Deirdre, Dulcie, Betty, and Barbara to follow; they were not going to be outdone in courage, and they felt that at any rate there was safety in numbers. There was nothing very terrible about the dining-room, in which they found themselves, it only looked miserable and forlorn, with the damp paper hanging in strips from the walls, and heaps of straw left by the remover's men strewn about the floor.

"We'll go and explore the rest of the house," said Annie, with a half-nervous chuckle. "Come along, anybody who's game!"

Nobody wished to remain behind alone, so they went all together, holding each other's arms, squealing, or gasping, or giggling, as occasion prompted. They peeped into the empty drawing-room and the silent kitchen, where the grate was red with rust; hurried past a dark hall cupboard, and found themselves at the foot of the staircase.

"Oh, I daren't go up; I simply daren't!" bleated Barbara piteously.

"Suppose the ghost lives up there?" suggested Betty.

"My good girl, no self-respecting spook likes to make an exhibition of itself," returned Annie. "The sight of six of us would scare it away. I don't mean to say I'd go alone, but now we're all here it's different."

"We've been more than Miss Harding's ten minutes," vacillated Deirdre.

"Oh, bother! One doesn't often get the chance to explore. Come along, you sillies, what are you frightened at?"

So together they mounted the stairs and took a hasty survey of the upper story. Here the remover's men had evidently done their work even more carelessly than down below, for though the furniture had been taken away, enough rubbish had been left to provide a rummage sale. All kinds of old articles not worth removing were lying where they had been thrown down on the bedroom floor—old curtains, old shoes, scraps of mouldy carpet, the laths of venetian blinds, broken lamp shades, empty bottles, torn magazines, cracked pottery, worn-out brushes, and decrepit straw palliasses.

"Did you ever see such an extraordinary conglomeration of queer things?" said Annie. "I wonder they didn't tidy the house up before they went. No wonder nobody would take it! And look, girls! They've actually left a whole bathful of old letters! Somebody has begun to tear them up, and not finished. They ought to have burnt them. Just look at this piece! It has a lovely crest on it."

"Oh, has it? Give it to me; I'm collecting crests," cried Deirdre, commandeering the scrap of paper. "It's a jolly one, too. I say, are there any more? Move out, Annie, and let me see!"

"Look here," remonstrated Barbara; "I don't think we ought to go rummaging amongst old letters. It doesn't seem quite—quite honourable, does it? They are not ours, Annie. I wish you'd stop! No, Gerda, don't look at them, please! Oh, I say, I wish you'd all come away! Let's go. Miss Harding will think we're drowned in the river, or something; and at any rate she'll scold us no end for being so long. Do you know the time?"

There was certainly force in Barbara's remarks. Their ten minutes' leave had exceeded half an hour, and Miss Harding would undoubtedly require a substantial reason for their delay.

"Oh, goody! It's four o'clock!" chirruped Betty. "I'd no idea it was so late! We don't want to get into a row with Miss Birks. I believe I hear Romola shouting in the road. They've come to look for us!"

"We'd best scoot, then," said Annie, and flinging back the letters into the bath, she turned with the rest and clattered downstairs.

Miss Harding, grave, annoyed, and justly indignant, was waiting for them on the bridge. She received them with the scolding they merited.

"Where have you been, you naughty, naughty girls? You're not to be trusted a minute out of my sight! I gave you permission to go straight to the bottom of the hill and back, and here you've been away more than half an hour! What were you doing in that garden? You had no right there! Come along this instant and walk before me, two and two. Miss Birks will have to hear about this. A nice report to take back of your afternoon's work at map drawing!"

Map drawing! They had forgotten all about the maps. The girls looked at one another, conscience-stricken; and Deirdre, with an awful pang, realized that she had left her note-book on the mantelpiece of the dining-room. She had been disposed to titter before, but she felt now that the affair was no joking matter.

"Miss Harding mustn't know we've been inside the house," she whispered to Gerda, with whom in the hurry of the moment she had paired off.

"No one's likely to tell her, and she couldn't see us come out of the window from where she was standing," returned Gerda.

"We shall get into trouble enough as it is. I didn't think Miss Harding would have cut up so rough about it. I say, just think of leaving those old letters all lying about! I got one—at least it's a scrap of one—with a lovely crest, a boar's head and a lot of stars—all in gold."

"What!" gasped Gerda. "Did you say you found that on a letter?"

"Well, it's a piece of a letter, anyway."

"Oh, do let me see it!"

"Is Miss Harding looking? Well, here it is. Be careful! She's got her eye on us! Oh, give it me back, quick!"

Gerda had turned the scrap of paper over and was glancing at the writing on the other side. She reddened with annoyance as Deirdre snatched back her treasure.

"Let me see it again!" she pleaded.

"No, no; it's safe in my pocket! Better not run any risks."

"You might give it to me. I'm collecting crests."

"A likely idea! Do you think, if I wanted to part with it, I'd present it to you? No, I mean to keep it myself, thanks."

"I'd buy it, if you like."

"I don't sell my things."

"Not if I offered something nice?"

"Not for anything you'd offer me," returned Deirdre, whose temper was in a touchy condition, and her spirit of opposition thoroughly aroused. "We don't haggle over our things at the Dower House, whatever you may do in Germany."

Gerda said no more at the time, but at night in their bedroom she returned once more to the subject.

"You won't get it if you bother me to the end of the term," declared Deirdre, locking up the bone of contention in her jewel-case and putting the key in her pocket.

"What do you want it for so particularly, Gerda?" asked Dulcie sharply.

"Oh, nothing! Only a fancy of my own," replied Gerda, reddening with one of her sudden fits of blushing, as she turned to the dressing-table and began to comb her flaxen hair.

CHAPTER VI

Ragtime

IF there was one thing more than another that the girls of the Dower House considered a particular and pressing grievance it was a wet Saturday afternoon. They were all of them outdoor enthusiasts, and to be obliged to stop in the house instead of tramping the moors or roaming on the sea-shore was regarded as a supreme penance. On the Saturday following the mapping expedition there was no mistake about the rain—it seemed to come down in a solid sheet from a murky sky, which offered absolutely no prospect of clearing.

The overflowing gutter-pipes emptied veritable rivulets into a temporary pond on the front drive; the lawn appeared fast turning into a morass; and even indoors the atmosphere was so soaked with damp that a dewy film covered banisters, furniture, and woodwork, and the wall-paper on the stairs distinctly changed its hue. In VB classroom the girls hung about disconsolately. There was to have been a special fossil foray that afternoon under the leadership of a lady from Perranwrack, who took an interest in the school, and who had thrown out hints of a fire of driftwood and a picnic tea among the rocks.

"It's so particularly aggravating, because Miss Hall has to go up to London on Monday and won't be back for weeks, so probably she won't be able to arrange to take us again this term," grumbled Romola.

"It's too—too *triste*!" murmured Deirdre in a die-away voice, arranging a cushion behind her head with elaborate show of indolence.

"Weally wetched!" echoed Dulcie lackadaisically, sinking into the basket-chair with an even more used-up air than her chum.

"Good old second best!" laughed Betty. "Whom are you both copying now? Have you been gobbling a surreptitious penny novelette? I can generally tell your course of reading from your poses. These present airs and graces suggest some such title as 'Lady Rosamond's Mystery' or 'The

Earl's Secret'. Confess, now, you're imagining yourselves members of the aristocracy."

"I believe the penny novelettes are invariably written in top garrets by people who've never even had a nodding acquaintance with dukes and duchesses," said Barbara. "The real article's very different from the 'belted earl' of fiction. The Clara-Vere-de-Vere type is extinct now. If you were a genuine countess, Deirdre, you'd probably be addressing hundreds of envelopes in aid of a philanthropic society, instead of lounging there looking like a dying duck in a thunderstorm. Don't glare! I speak the solemn words of truth."

"You make my he—head ache," protested Deirdre with half-closed eyelids, but her complaint met with no sympathy. Instead, several strong and insistent hands pulled her forcibly out of her chair and flung away the cushion.

"I tell you we're sick of 'Lady Isobel' or whoever she may be. For goodness' sake be somebody more cheerful if you won't be yourself. Can't you get up an Irish mood for a change? A bit of the brogue would hearten up this clammy afternoon."

"Oh, isn't it piggy and nasty!" exclaimed Annie, stretching out her arms in the agony of an elephantine yawn. "I want my tea! I want my tea! I want my tea! And I shan't get it for a whole long weary hour!"

"Poor martyr! Here, squattez-ici on the hearth-rug and I'll make you a triscuit."

"What on earth is a triscuit?"

"Oh, you're not bright or you'd guess. It's a biscuit toasted nicely brown and eaten hot. Don't you twig? A biscuit means 'twice cooked'; therefore if it's cooked again it must be a triscuit. That stands to reason."

"Is it to be a barmecide feast? I don't see your precious biscuits."

"'"I've got 'un here," sez she, quite quiet-like,'" returned Betty, who was a Mrs. Ewing enthusiast, and quoted Dame Datchet with relish. "Half a pound of cream crackers, and I mean to be generous and share 'em round. Don't you all bless me? Now the question is, how we're going to 'triscuit' them."

The girls crowded round with suggestions. Toasting biscuits was certainly more entertaining than doing nothing. Deirdre forgot for the time that she was a heroine of fiction, and plumped down by the fender with a lack of high-born dignity that would have scandalized "Lady Isobel".

"You'll smash them up if you try sticking your penknife through them," she observed. "It'll burn your fingers too to hold them so close to the fire. Try the tongs."

"Some of them might be tilted up in the fender," volunteered Gerda, whose rare remarks were generally to the point. "They'd be getting hot, and we could finish them off afterwards."

"Right you are! Stick them up in a row. Now if I take this one with the tongs and hold it just over that red piece in the fire——"

"Be careful!"

"Remember it's fragile."

"There, I knew you'd smash it! Oh, pick the other half out, quick! It's burning!"

"What a Johnnie-fingers you are! It's done for."

In the end—and it was Gerda's quiet suggestion—the tongs were placed over the fire like a gridiron and the biscuits successfully popped on the top and turned when one side was done. Everybody appreciated them down to the last crumb, and awarded Betty a vote of thanks for her brilliant idea.

"The worst of it is, they're finished too soon," sighed Evie, "and we've nothing else to fill up the gap till tea-time. I want to do something outrageous—break a window or smash an ornament, or damage the furniture! What a nuisance conscience is! Why does the 'inward monitor' restrain me?"

"Probably the wholesome dread of consequences my dear. You might cut your hand in a wild orgy of window smashing and there'd be bills to pay afterwards for reglazing and medical attendance."

"But can't we do anything interesting?"

"Let's play a trick on V_A," suggested Annie. "It would do them good and shake them up. My conscience gives me full leave."

"It's celebrated for its well-known elasticity!" chuckled Evie.

"But what could we do?"

"Oh, just rag them a little somehow. It would be rather sport."

"Plans for sport in ragtime wanted! All offers carefully considered. Now, then, bring on your suggestions."

Everybody stared hopefully at everybody else, but no one rose to the occasion.

"Going—going—going—a first-rate opportunity for mirth-provoking ____"

"Could we get them into the passage and one of us hide behind the curtain of the barred room and act ghost?" proposed Romola desperately.

Her suggestion, however, was received with utter scorn.

"Can't you think of anything more original than that?"

"We're fed up with that ghost trick. Nobody even calls it funny now."

"Besides, Miss Birks said she'd punish anyone who did it again. She was awfully angry last time."

Duly squashed, Romola subsided, and the silence which followed resembled that of a Quakers' meeting.

"I've got it!" shouted Betty at last, clapping her hands ecstatically. "The very thing! Oh, the supremest joke!"

"Good biz! But please condescend to explain," commented Evie.

"Oh, we'll try thing-um-bob—what d'you call it? Mesmerism—that's the word I want. With dinner plates, you know."

Apparently nobody knew, for all looked interested and intelligent, but unenlightened.

"Do you mean to say you've never heard of it? Oh, goody! What luck!"

"Look here," interposed Annie, "you're not going to rag us as well. It's to be for the benefit of VA if there's any sell about it."

"All right! They'll really be enough, and you shall act audience. Only with fourteen of you it would have been so——"

"Betty Scott, give us your word this instant that you won't play tricks on your own Form."

"I won't—I won't—honest, I won't!"

"And tell us what you're going to do."

"No, that would spoil it all. You must wait and see. Barbara, go to the kitchen door and cajole Cook into lending us seven dinner plates. Say you'll pledge your honour not to break them. And purloin a candle from the lamp cupboard. Be as quick as you can! Time wanes."

Barbara executed her errand with speed and success. She soon returned with the plates and set them down on the table. Betty lighted the candle, laid one plate aside, then held each of the others in turn over the flame till the bottoms inside the rims were well coloured with smoke. The girls watched her curiously.

"Now, I'm ready!" she announced, "but I want a messenger. Elyned, you go and tap at VA door and say we shall be very pleased if they care to come and try a most interesting experiment. Mind you put it politely, and for your life don't snigger."

Now VA had been spending an even duller and more wearisome afternoon than VB, for they had not had the diversion of toasting biscuits. They were yawning in the last stages of boredom when Elyned arrived and delivered her message. Usually they considered themselves far too select to have much to do with the lower division, but to-day anything to break the monotony was welcome. They accepted the invitation with alacrity, and came trooping in to the rival classroom with pleased anticipation in their faces.

"It's a most curious experiment," began Betty. "I learnt it from a cousin who's been out East. He saw it practised by some Chinese priests at a josshouse. I believe it's one of the first steps of initiation in Esoteric

Buddhism. My cousin's not exactly a Theosophist, but he's interested in comparative theologies, and he went about with a lama, and found out ever so many of their secrets. He wrote down the formulary of this for me."

"What's it about?" asked the elder girls, looking considerably impressed.

"It's a species of mesmerism—or animal magnetism, as some people prefer to call it. You make certain passes, and repeat certain words after me, and then you all get into the hypnotic state. Of course it depends how psychic you are, but anybody with even undeveloped mediumistic powers will sometimes give replies to questions they couldn't possibly answer in the normal state."

"I suppose it won't hurt us?" asked Agnes Gillard rather gravely.

"Oh, not at all! It's wonderful sometimes to find how people who've never even suspected they possessed psychic gifts bring out absolutely unaccountable pieces of information. It really would be quite uncanny, except for the latest theory that it's merely utilizing a natural power once cultivated by man, but long forgotten except by a few priests in the Tibetan monasteries. The Theosophical Society, of course, is trying to revive it."

"I'm afraid I don't know anything about Theosophy," murmured Hilda Marriott.

"It's akin to the Eleusinian mysteries and the cult of Isis," continued Betty unblushingly. "You have to understand 'Karma' (that's reincarnation) and 'Yoga' (that's flitting about in your astral body while you're asleep), and—and—" But here both memory and invention failed her, so she hurriedly changed her point. "Oh! it would take me years to explain, and you couldn't understand unless you'd been initiated. Let's get to the experiment. Will you all stand in a row?"

"Aren't any of you going to try?" asked Irene Jordan, addressing the members of VB, who, solemn as judges, stood slightly in the background.

"We can only do it with seven, the mystic number—and there are eight of them, and they can't agree who's to be left out," said Betty hurriedly. "It's always done with six neophytes and one initiated. If you're ready, we'd best begin, and not waste any more time."

She arranged her neophytes in a line, and gave to each a plate, telling her to hold it firmly in the left hand. Then, taking her stand facing them, she raised her own plate to the level of her chest.

"Now you must do exactly as I do!" she commanded. "All fix your eyes on me, and don't take them off me for a single instant. The concentration of the seven visual currents is of vital importance. Put the middle finger of the right hand beneath the plate exactly in the centre, then describe a circle with it on the under side of the plate. Be sure the circle follows the same course as the sun, or we may break the mesmeric current. Watch what I'm doing. Now describe a circle on your face in the same manner, beginning with the left cheek. Copy me carefully. And now we must repeat the cabalistic formulary (the oldest in the world—Solomon got it from El Zenobi, the chief of the Genii): 'Om mani padme hum'. Let us say it slowly all together seven times, performing the orthodox circles at each."

The neophytes played their parts admirably. They never removed their gaze from the face of their instructress; they copied her every movement, and repeated the mystic words to the very best of their ability. "Om mani padme hum" rolled from their lips seven times, and seemed to suggest the dreamy atmosphere of the occult.

"The mesmeric current is forming! I can feel it working!" declared Betty. "It only requires further visualization for the hypnotic state to follow. To complete the magnetic circle, will you all kindly turn and face each other?"

Still holding the plates, the obedient six swung round, stared at one another, then gasped and shrieked. And well they might, for, one and all, their countenances were besmirched with black in a series of concentric rings which caused them to resemble Zulu chiefs or American-Indian warriors on the warpath.

"Oh! oh! oh!" came from the members of VB, who, having been stationed behind the neophytes, had been in equal ignorance of the trick that was being played on them. Then everybody exploded.

"Oh, you look so funny!"

"Is the magnetic current working?"

"Is it the cult of Isis?"

"Oh, my heart! Oh! ho! ho!" gurgled Betty. "You didn't twig your plates were smoked and mine wasn't! Oh, I've done you! Done you brown, literally!"

"You p-p-p-pig!" spluttered the victims.

"Don't break the plates! Here, put them on the table! Oh, don't look so indignant, or you'll kill me! I've got a stitch in my side with laughing. Here, don't stalk off like offended zebras! I'll apologize! I'll go down on my bended knees! It was a brutal rag—yes—yes—I own up frankly! I'll grovel! *Peccavi! Peccavi! Miserere mei!*"

"I've got some chocolates here," murmured Annie Pridwell. "I was keeping them for Sunday, but do have them," handing the packet round among the outraged upper division.

The occasion certainly seemed to warrant some form of compensation. Evie hastily followed Annie's example, and sacrificed a private store of toffee on the altar of hospitality. Blissfully sucking, the six seniors allowed themselves to be mollified. As connoisseurs of jokes, they were ready to acknowledge the superior excellence of the trick played upon them; moreover, they found one another's appearance highly diverting.

"Betty Scott, you'll be the death of me some day," remarked Rhoda Wilkins. "Oh, Agnes! If you could only see yourself in the glass!"

"It's the pot calling the kettle! Look at your own face!"

"Do you think we could possibly work it on the Sixth?"

"No, they'd smell a rat."

"I want my tea," said Annie. "Oh, cock-a-doodle-doo! There's the first bell! Hip-hip-hooray! I say, you six, if you don't want to give Miss Birks a first-class fit, you'd best be toddling to the bath-room, and applying the soap-and-water treatment to your interesting countenances."

CHAPTER VII

An Invitation

"Zickery, dickery, lumby tum,Tip me the wink, and out I'll come,Leave my pagoda so glum, glum, glum,To drink green tea with my own Yum-Yum!"

So chanted Evie Bennett on the following Monday, bursting into VB room with a face betokening news, and a manner suggestive of Bedlam.

"What's the matter, you lunatic? Look here, if you go on like a dancing dervish we shall have to provide you with a padded room! Mind the inkpot! Oh, I say, you'll have the black-board over! Hasn't anybody got a strait-waistcoat? Evie's gone sheer, stark, raving mad!"

"I've got news, my hearty! News! news! news!

'What will you take for my news?I know it will make you enthuse!There isn't a girl who'll refuse,Or offer to make an excuse.'

Ahem! A poor thing, but mine own. I'm waxing so poetical, I think I must be inspired."

"Or possessed! Sit down, you mad creature, and talk sense. What's your precious news?"

"Mrs. Trevellyan requests the pleasure of the company of the young ladies of Miss Birks's seminary to drink tea with her on the occasion of the natal day of her nephew, Master Ronald Trevellyan," announced Evie, changing suddenly to a ceremonious eighteenth-century manner, and dropping a stiff curtsy.

"Ronnie's birthday!"

"Oh, what sport!"

"It's on Wednesday."

"Has she asked only us?"

"No, the whole school is to go, mistresses and all," returned Evie. "Mrs. Trevellyan wants to introduce Ronnie's new governess to us."

"There are sure to be games, and perhaps a competition with prizes," rejoiced Annie Pridwell; "and we always have delicious teas at the Castle. Gerda Thorwaldson, why don't you look pleased? You take it as quietly as if it were a parochial meeting. What a mum mouse you are!"

"Is it anything to get so excited over?" replied Gerda calmly.

"Of course it is! The Castle's the Castle, and Mrs. Trevellyan is—well, just Mrs. Trevellyan. There are the loveliest things there—foreign curiosities, and old pictures, and illuminated books, and we're allowed to look at them; and there's special preserved ginger from China, and boxes of real Eastern Turkish Delight. Oh, it's a fairy palace! You may thank your stars you're going!"

In spite of Annie's transports, Gerda did not look particularly delighted. She only smiled in a rather sickly fashion, and said nothing. The others, however, were much too occupied with their own pleasurable expectations to take any notice of her lack of enthusiasm. They had accepted her quiet ways as part of herself, and had set her down as a not very interesting addition to the Form, and thought her opinions—if indeed she possessed any—were of scant importance.

Gerda had made very little headway with her companions; her intense reserve seemed to set a barrier between them and herself, and after one or two efforts at being friendly the girls had given her up, and took no more trouble over her. "Gerda the Silent," "The Recluse," "The Oyster," were some of the names by which she was known, and she certainly justified every item of her reputation for reticence. If she did not talk much, she was, however, a good listener. Nothing in the merry chat of the schoolroom escaped her, and anybody who had been curious enough to watch her carefully might have noticed that often, when seemingly buried in a book, her eyes did not move over the page, and all her attention was given to the conversation that was going on in her vicinity.

Having received an invitation to Ronnie's birthday party, of course the burning subject of discussion was what to give him as a present. Miss Birks vetoed the idea of each girl making a separate offering, and suggested a general subscription list to buy one handsome article.

"It will be quite sufficient, and I am sure Mrs. Trevellyan would far rather have it so," she decreed.

"It's too bad, for I'd made up my mind to give him a box of soldiers," complained Annie, in private.

"And I'd a book in my eye," said Elyned.

"Perhaps Miss Birks is right," said Romola, "because, you see, some of us might give nicer presents than the others, and perhaps there'd be a little jealousy; and at any rate, comparisons are odious."

"Miss Birks has limited the subscriptions to a shilling each," commented Deirdre.

"Then let's take our list now. I'll write down our names, and you can tell me the amounts."

For such an object everyone was disposed to be liberal—everyone, that is to say, except Gerda Thorwaldson. When she was applied to, she flatly refused.

"Don't you want to join in the present to Ronnie?" gasped Romola, in utter amazement.

"Why should I?"

"Why, because we're going to tea at the Castle; and Ronnie is Ronnie, and Mrs. Trevellyan will be pleased too!"

"I don't know Mrs. Trevellyan."

"Well, you soon will. You'll be introduced to her on Wednesday. She always says something nice to new girls—asks them where their homes are, and if they've brothers and sisters, and how old they are—and if she finds out she knows their parents or their friends she's so interested. And she has such a good memory for faces! She actually recognized Irene Jordan, although she'd never seen her in her life before, because Irene is so like an aunt, a Miss Jordan who is a friend of Mrs. Trevellyan's."

Gerda had turned a dull crimson at these remarks. She kept her eyes fixed on the floor, and made no reply. What her inward thoughts might be, no one could fathom.

"Isn't your name to go down at all, then, on the list?" asked Romola, with considerable impatience.

"No, thanks!" replied Gerda briefly, turning awkwardly away.

Wednesday arrived, and perhaps even Ronnie hardly welcomed his birthday more than did his friends at the Dower House. His present—a toy circus—had arrived, and had been on exhibition in Miss Birks's study, and everybody had agreed that it was the very thing to please him. At three o'clock the girls went to change their school dresses for more festive attire, and were more than ordinarily particular in their choice of preparations.

"How slow you are, Gerda Thorwaldson!" said Deirdre, whose own immaculate toilet was complete. "You haven't put on your dress yet. Why don't you hurry?"

"You needn't think we'll wait for you," added Dulcie.

Instead of replying, Gerda calmly donned her dressing-gown, and, volunteering no explanation, went out of the room and shut the door behind her.

She walked downstairs to Miss Birks's study, and, tapping at the door, reported herself.

"May I, please, stay at home this afternoon?" she begged. "I'm afraid I don't feel up to going out to tea to-day."

"Not go to the Castle? My dear child, I hope you're not ill? Certainly stay at home, and lie down on your bed if your head aches. Nettie shall bring your tea upstairs. I'm sorry you'll miss so great a treat as a visit to Mrs. Trevellyan's."

Gerda made no comment; but as she was habitually sparing of speech, her silence did not strike Miss Birks as anything unusual. It was time to start, and the Principal had her nineteen other pupils to think about, so she dismissed the pseudo-invalid with a final injunction to rest.

Gerda did not return to her bedroom till she was perfectly sure that Deirdre and Dulcie had left it. She had no wish to run the gauntlet of their inevitable criticisms, or to be questioned too closely on the nature of her sudden indisposition. She loitered about the upper landing until from the end window she saw the whole school—girls, mistresses, and Principal—file down the drive and out through the gate in the direction of the Castle. Then, going to her dormitory, she rang the bell, and lay down on her bed.

"Would you mind bringing my cup of tea now, Nettie, please?" she asked, when the housemaid appeared. "And then I should like to be left perfectly quiet until the others come back."

"Of course I'll bring it, miss," said the sympathetic Nettie. "Nothing like a cup of tea for a headache. The kettle's on the boil, so you can have it at once. I won't be more than a minute or two fetching it"

Nettie was as prompt as her word. She returned almost directly with the tea, and arranged it temptingly on a little table by the bedside.

"Shut your eyes and try and go to sleep when you've drunk it," she recommended. "You'll perhaps wake up quite fresh. It is a pity you couldn't go with the other young ladies to the Castle. They were all so full of it—and Master Ronnie's birthday, too! I know how disappointed you must feel."

Gerda finished her tea far more rapidly than is usual for invalids with sick-headaches; then, instead of taking Nettie's advice and closing her eyes, she rose and put on her school dress, her coat, and her cap. She opened the door and listened—not a sound was to be heard. The servants must surely be having their own tea in the kitchen, and no one else was in the house. With extreme caution she crept along the passage and down the stairs. The side door was open, and as quietly as a shadow she passed out and dodged round the corner of the house. A few minutes later she was running, running at the very top of her speed across the warren in the direction of a certain rocky creek not far from St. Perran's well.

When the girls returned at half-past six, full of their afternoon's experiences, they found Gerda lying on her bed, with the blind drawn down. There was an almost feverish colour in her cheeks.

"We'd a ripping time!" Dulcie assured her. "A splendid 'Natural Objects' competition. I nearly got a prize, but I put 'snake-skin' down for one, and it was really a piece of the skin of a finnan-haddock. Emily Northwood won the first, with sixteen objects right out of twenty, and Hilda Marriott was second with fourteen. I might have known that specimen was fish scales.

"Ronnie was delighted with his circus," added Dulcie. "He gave us each a kiss all round. And Mrs. Trevellyan was so nice! She was sorry you couldn't come, and hoped she'd see you some other time. By the by, how's your headache?"

"Rather better. I think I'll get up now," murmured Gerda. "I haven't touched my Latin to-day."

"Plucky of you to come and do prep. If I had a headache, wouldn't I just make it an excuse to knock off Virgil!"

It was getting near to the end of February. The days were lengthening visibly, and the sun, which only a month ago had appeared every morning like a red ball over the hill behind the Castle, now rose, bright and shining, a long way to eastward. In spite of occasional spring storms, the weather was on the whole mild, and every day fresh flowers were pushing up in the school garden. The warren, attractive even in winter, was doubly delightful now primrose tufts were venturing to show among the last year's bracken, and the gorse was beginning to gleam golden in sheltered stretches. The girls were out every available moment of their spare time, rambling over the headland or haunting the sea-shore. For most of them the latter provided the greater entertainment.

They had discovered a new occupation, that of salvaging the driftwood, and found it so enthralling that for the present it overtopped all other amusements. The high spring-tides and occasional storms washed up quantities of pieces of timber, and to rescue these from the edge of the waves, and carry them into a place of safety, became as keen a sport as fishing. Quite a little wood-stack was accumulating under the cliff, and the girls had designs of carrying it piece by piece to a point on the top of the headland, and there building a beacon of noble proportions to be fired on Empire Day amid suitable rejoicings.

It was exciting work to skip about at the water's edge, grasping at bits of old spars or shattered boards. The sea seemed to enjoy the fun, and would bob them near and snatch them away in tantalizing fashion, sometimes adding a wetting as a point to the joke. To secure a fine piece of wood without getting into the water was the triumph of skill, attended with considerable risk, not to life or limb, but to length of recreation, for

Miss Birks had laid down an inviolable rule that anybody who got her feet wet at this occupation must immediately return to school, change shoes and stockings, and desist from further attempts on that day. One or two of the girls were lucky enough to possess india-rubber wading boots, with which they could venture to defy Father Ocean and rob him of some of the choicest of his spoils, but they were the highly-favoured few; the rank and file had to content themselves with the ordinary method of swift snatching with the aid of a hockey stick.

Two days after Ronnie's birthday party a strong wind and squall during the night had furnished material for more than usually good sport, and the whole school betook itself to the beach to try to reap a harvest. Laughing, joking, squealing, the girls pursued their quarry, enjoying the fun all the more for the accidents of the moment. Evie Bennett dropped her hockey stick, and nearly lost it altogether. Romola Harvey slipped and fell flat into a pool of water; and many other minor mishaps occurred to keep up the excitement until the catch of the year was secured, a large piece of timber which it took the united efforts of all arms to drag successfully up the beach. Deirdre and Dulcie at last, grown reckless ventured a risky experiment on their own account, with the result that a wave caught them neatly, and gave them the full benefit of sea-water treatment.

"Oh, you're done for. Go back at once!" commanded Jessie Macpherson, the head girl, whose office it was to see that the rule about changing shoes was duly observed.

"Sea-water doesn't hurt," protested the chums.

"Your feet are wet through, so back you trot this instant. Do you want me to report you?"

Very loath to leave the shore, Deirdre and Dulcie were nevertheless bound to obey, so they toiled regretfully up the steep path from the cove, casting a lingering eye on their companions, who were still hard at work.

"Where's Gerda?" asked Dulcie. "She's not down there, and now I think of it, I haven't seen her for the last half-hour or more. Did she get wet?"

"I really didn't notice. I suppose she must have, and been sent back. We shall probably find her in the garden."

The two stepped briskly over the warren, their shoes drying on their feet with a rapidity which made them disparage Miss Birks's excellent rule about changing.

"It's just her fuss—we should have taken no harm," said Deirdre. "I say, surely that's Ronnie's laugh. I'd know it anywhere. Where is the child?"

The girls were passing close to the high wall which separated the Castle grounds from the warren, and as it seemed more than probable that Ronnie was inside, playing in the garden, they managed with considerable effort, and the aid of some strong ivy, to climb to the top and peep over. Here a most unexpected sight met their gaze.

On the grass, under a tamarisk bush, sat Gerda with Ronnie on her knee. She had evidently made friends with the little fellow to a great extent, for he seemed very much at home with her, and the two were laughing and joking together in the most intimate fashion. It was such an absolutely new aspect of Gerda that Deirdre and Dulcie were dumb with amazement. When, at the Dower House, had she laughed so gaily, or talked in so animated and sprightly a fashion? No shy, reserved, taciturn recluse this; her eyes were shining, and her whole face was full of a bright expression, such as the others had never seen there before.

"Hallo, Gerda! What are you doing here?" called Deirdre, finding speech at last.

Gerda dropped Ronnie, and sprang to her feet with a sharp exclamation. No one could have looked more utterly and egregiously caught. She stood staring at the two faces on the top of the wall, and offered no explanation whatever. Ronnie, however, waved his hand merrily.

"We've been playing Zoo," he volunteered. "Gerda's been a lion, and gobbled me up, and she's been an elephant and given me rides, and we were both polar bears, and growled at each other. Listen how I can growl now—Ur-ur-ugh! Oh, and look what she's given me for my birthday! It comes from Germany," producing from his pocket a little compass. "Now if ever I get lost, I can always find my way home. See, I can show you which is north, and south, and east, and west."

"You'd better be going back, Gerda," remarked Dulcie grimly. "You know we're not allowed in the Castle grounds without a special invitation."

"I'll come through the side gate," replied Gerda, turning from Ronnie without even a good-bye. Deirdre and Dulcie dropped from the wall, and met their room-mate at the identical moment when she passed through the turnstile.

"Well, of all mean people you're the meanest!" observed Deirdre. "I call it sneaky to take such an advantage, and go to play with Ronnie by yourself. We'd do it if it were allowed, but it isn't."

"I wonder his governess wasn't with him," said Dulcie. "He's generally so very much looked after."

"And as for going inside the Castle garden, it was most fearful cheek," continued Deirdre. "We, who know Mrs. Trevellyan quite well, never think of doing such a thing."

"What I call meanest," put in Dulcie, "was to try and curry favour with Ronnie by giving him a birthday present on your own account. Miss Birks said there were to be no separate presents: we were all to join, so that there'd be no jealousy—and you wouldn't subscribe. Oh, you are a nasty, hole-and-corner, underhand sneak! Have you anything to say for yourself?"

But Gerda stumped resolutely along with her hands in her coat pockets, and answered never a word.

CHAPTER VIII

A Meeting on the Shore

"D'YOU know, Dulcie," remarked Deirdre, when the chums were alone, "the more I think about it, the more convinced I am there's something queer about Gerda Thorwaldson."

"So am I," returned Dulcie emphatically. "Something very queer indeed. I never liked her from the first: she always gives me the impression that she's listening and taking mental notes."

"For what?"

"Ah, that's the question! What?"

"I certainly think we ought to be on our guard, and to watch her carefully, only we mustn't on any account let her know what we're doing."

"Rather not!"

"She's no business to sneak away by herself when we're all salvaging on the beach. She knows perfectly well it's against rules."

"She doesn't seem to mind rules."

"Well, look here, we must keep an eye on her, and next time we see her decamping we'll just follow her, and watch where she goes. I don't like people with underhand ways."

"It doesn't suit us at the Dower House," agreed Dulcie.

Though the chums kept Gerda's movements under strict surveillance for several days, they could discover nothing at which to take exception. She did not attempt to absent herself, or in any way break rules; she asked no questions, and exhibited no curiosity on any subject. If possible, she was even more silent and self-contained than before. Rather baffled, the girls nevertheless did not relax their vigilance.

"She's foxing. We must wait and see what happens. Don't on any account let her humbug us," said Deirdre.

One afternoon a strong west wind blowing straight from the sea seemed to promise such a good haul at their engrossing occupation that the girls, who for a day or two had forsaken salvaging in favour of hockey practice, turned their steps one and all towards the beach. As they walked along across the warren they had a tolerably clear and uninterrupted view of the whole of the little peninsula, and were themselves very conspicuous objects to anyone who chanced to be walking on the shore. Deirdre's eyes were wandering from sea to sky, from distant rock to near primrose clumps, when, happening to glance in the direction of the cliff that overtopped St. Perran's well, she was perfectly sure that she saw a white handkerchief waved in the breeze. It was gone in an instant, and there was no sign of a human figure to account for the circumstance, but Deirdre was certain it was no illusion. She called Dulcie's attention to it, but Dulcie had been looking the other way, and had seen nothing.

"Probably it was only a piece of paper blowing down the cliff," she objected. "How could it be anyone waving? Nobody's allowed on the warren."

"It might be Ronnie and Miss Herbert."

"Oh no! We could see them quite plainly if it were."

"Gerda, did you notice something white?"

"I don't see anything there," replied Gerda, surveying the distance with her usual inscrutable expression. "I think you must have been mistaken."

It seemed quite a small and trivial matter, and though Deirdre, for the mere sake of argument, stuck to her point all the way down to the beach, the others only laughed at her.

"You'll be saying it's a ghost next," declared Betty. "I think you're blessed with a very powerful imagination, Deirdre."

Arrived on the shore, the girls found their expectations fully justified. Several most interesting-looking pieces of driftwood were bobbing about just at the edge of the waves, and with a little clever management could probably be secured, and would make a valuable addition to the stack which was to furnish their beacon fire. Jessie Macpherson, who possessed a pair of wading boots, was soon in command, directing the others how to act so that none of the flotsam should be lost, and marshalling her band of eager volunteers with the skill of a coastguardsman.

"Wait for the next big wave! Have your hockey sticks ready! Doris and Francie and I will wade in and try to catch it, then, when the wave's going back, you must all make a rush and try to hold it. Not this wave! Wait for that huge one that's coming. Are you ready? Now! Now!"

The owners of the wading boots did their duty nobly. They caught at the floating piece of timber and held on to it grimly, while a line of girls followed the retreating wave, and, making a dash, seized the trophy, and rolled it into safety.

"Oh, it's a gorgeous big one—the largest we have!"

"That was neatly done!"

"We've robbed old Father Neptune this time!"

"It's a piece of luck!"

"Of flotsam, you mean!"

"Three cheers for the beacon!"

"Hip, hip, hip, hooray!"

"Hooray! Hooray!" echoed Dulcie, then she looked round, and suddenly touched Deirdre on the arm.

In the midst of the general excitement Gerda had vanished. Where had she gone? That was the question which the chums at once asked each other. It was impossible that in so short a space of time she could have scaled the steep path from the cove on to the top of the cliff. She must surely have run along the shore instead. To the east the great mass of crags formed an impassable barrier, but it was just practicable to round the headland to the west. Without a moment's delay they dashed off in that direction. They tore in hot haste over the wet sand, scrambled anyhow amongst the seaweed-covered rocks at the point, regardless of injury to clothing, and, valiantly leaping a narrow channel, turned the corner, and found themselves in a second cove, similar to the former, but larger and more inaccessible from the cliffs. They were rewarded for their promptitude, as the first sight that caught their eyes was Gerda, speeding along several hundred yards in front of them, as if she had some definite object in view.

"Shall I shout after her?" gasped Dulcie.

"Not for the world," returned Deirdre. "We mustn't let her know she's being followed."

"If she looks back, she'll see us."

"We'll hide behind this rock."

"She'll be round the next corner in a minute."

"So she will. Then, look here, we must wait till she's gone, and then climb up the cliff, and run along and peep over from the top."

"Whew! It'll be a climb."

"Never mind, we'll manage it. Let us take off our coats and carry them. I'm so hot."

Deirdre's precautions proved to be most necessary. Gerda turned at the far headland, and took a survey of the bay before she scrambled round the point. She did not see the two heads peeping at her from behind the big rock, and, apparently, was satisfied that she had eluded pursuit. No sooner had she disappeared than Deirdre and Dulcie hurried forth, and, choosing what looked like a sheep track as the best substitute for a path, began their steep and toilsome climb. Excitement and determination spurred them on, and they persevered in spite of grazed knees and scratched fingers. Over jagged pieces of rock, between brambles that seemed set with more than their due share of thorns, catching on to tufts of grass or projecting roots for support, up they scrambled somehow, till they gained the level of the warren above.

The course that followed was a neat little bit of scouting. Making a bee-line for the next cove, they then dropped on their hands and knees, and, crawling under cover of the gorse bushes to the verge of the cliff, peeped cautiously over. Gerda was just below them, standing at the edge of the waves and looking out to sea. This creek was a much smaller and narrower one than the others, and the rocks were too precipitous to offer foothold even to the most venturesome climber.

Well concealed beneath a thick bush that overhung the brow of the crag, Deirdre and Dulcie had an excellent view of their schoolmate's movements without fear of betraying their presence. Gerda stood for a moment or two gazing at the water, then she gave a long and peculiar whistle, not unlike the cry of the curlew. It was at once answered by a similar one from a distance, and in the course of a few minutes a small white dinghy shot round the point from the west. It was rowed by a big, fine-looking, fair-haired man, who wore a brown knitted jersey and no hat.

With powerful strokes he pulled himself along, till, reaching the shallows, he shipped his oars, jumped overboard, and ran his little craft upon the beach. He had scarcely stepped out of the water before Gerda was at his side, and the two walked together along the beach, he apparently asking eager questions, to which she gave swift replies. Up and down, up and down for fully ten minutes they paced, too absorbed in their conversation to look up at the cliff above, though had they done so they would scarcely have spied the two spectators who cowered close under the shelter of the overhanging hazel bush, squeezing each others' hands in the excitement of the scene they were witnessing.

The man appeared to have many directions to give, for he talked long and earnestly, and Gerda nodded her head frequently, as if to show her thorough comprehension of what he was saying. At last she glanced at her watch, and they both hurried back to where they had left the boat. He launched his little dinghy, sprang in, seized the oars, and rowed away as rapidly as he had arrived. Gerda stood on the beach looking after him till he had rounded the point and disappeared from her view, then, crying bitterly, she began to walk back in the direction from which she had come. Deirdre and Dulcie waited until she was safely past the corner and out of sight, then they sprang up and stretched their cramped limbs, for the discomfort of their position had grown wellnigh intolerable.

"Ugh! I don't believe I could have kept still one second longer," exploded Dulcie.

"My feet are full of pins and needles," said Deirdre, stamping her hardest, "and my elbow is so sore where I have been leaning on it, I can't tell you how it hurts."

"It can't be worse than mine."

"I say, though, we've seen something queer!"

"Rather!"

"Who can that man be?"

"That's just what I want to know."

"It looks very suspicious."

"Suspicious isn't the name for it. Do you think we ought to tell Miss Birks?"

"No, no, no! That would never do. We must say nothing at all, but go on keeping our eyes open, and see if we can find out anything more. Don't let Gerda get the least hint that we're on her track."

"Suppose Jessie asks us why we left the cove? What are we to say?"

"Why, that we missed Gerda, and as she's our room-mate, we went over the warren to see if we could find her and make a threesome. It was our plain duty."

Dulcie chuckled.

"Oh, our duty, of course! And naturally, of course, we didn't find her on the warren. She wasn't there."

"She'll have to make her own explanations if Jessie asks her where she was."

"Trust her for that!"

"I wonder what excuse she'll give?"

As it happened, everything turned out most simply. Deirdre and Dulcie overtook Gerda farther on along the warren, and concluded that she had probably climbed up from the second cove by the same path as themselves. They discreetly ignored her red eyes and made some casual remarks upon the weather. The three were walking together when the rest of the school came up from salvaging. The head girl looked at them, but seeing that they formed an orthodox "threesome" made no comment, and passed on. She probably thought they had been taking a stroll on the warren. Gerda looked almost gratefully at her companions. She had evidently felt afraid lest they should mention the fact that she had not been with them the whole time. She made quite an effort to speak on indifferent subjects as they walked back, and was more conversational than they ever remembered her. At tea-time, however, she relapsed into silence, and during the evening nobody could draw a word from her. Dulcie woke once during the night, and heard her crying quietly.

The two chums puzzled their heads continually over the meaning of the strange scene they had witnessed. Many were the theories they advanced and cast aside. One only appeared to Deirdre to be a really possible explanation.

"I'll tell you what I believe," she said, "I think that man in the brown jersey is a German spy. You know, although Gerda sticks to it that she is English, we've always had our doubts. She looks German, and she speaks better German than Mademoiselle, though Mademoiselle's Swiss, and has talked two languages from babyhood. Gerda isn't an English name. She says it was taken from Gerda in 'The Snow Queen', but can one believe her? I'm called 'Deirdre' because my family's Irish, and it's an old Celtic name, but 'Gerda' is distinctly Teutonic. Then she spells Thorwaldson 'son' but in one of her books I found it written Thorwaldsen, which is most suggestive. No, mark my words, she's a German, and she's come here as a spy."

"What has she to spy on?" asked Dulcie, deeply impressed.

"Why, don't you see? A knowledge of this part of the coast would be simply invaluable to the Germans, if they wanted to invade us. All these narrow creeks and coves would be places to bring vessels to and land troops, and the Castle could be taken and held as a fort, and perhaps the Dower House too."

"Is that why she was measuring the passage?"

"It might very easily be! She'd give them a plan of the school."

"Oh! Would they come and turn us out and kill us?"

"One never knows what an enemy might do. This bit of shore is not at all well protected; we're a long way from a coastguard station on either side. It's just the sort of spot where a whole army could be quietly landed in a few hours, before anyone had an inkling of what was going on. There's no doubt that we ought to watch Gerda most carefully. It may mean saving our country from a terrible catastrophe."

CHAPTER IX

A Message

Now that they had decided on an explanation of their schoolfellow's mysterious conduct, the chums felt that every circumstance seemed to point in its favour. They wondered they had never thought of it before. The importance of keeping a strict watch was realized by both. There was a certain satisfaction in doing so. They felt as if they were rendering their country a service, almost indeed as if they were members of a secret diplomatic corps, and had been told off for special duty. Who knew what England might have to thank them for some day? Possibly at no very far-off date the whole country might be ringing with their names, and the newspapers publishing portraits of the two schoolgirls who had averted a national disaster. Just to be prepared for emergencies, they took snapshots of each other with Dulcie's Brownie camera, and added a series of photographs of the school, all of which they thought would be very suitable to give to the enthusiastic reporter who would demand an illustrated interview. They were rather disappointed with the results of the portraits, which in their estimation scarcely did them justice.

"I look more like forty than fourteen!" said Deirdre, regarding ruefully the dark shadows on her cheeks and the lines under her eyes. "It doesn't show my hair properly, either. No one could tell it was curly."

"And I look as fat as a prize pig, with no eyes to speak of, and an imbecile grin."

"I wonder how real photographers manage to touch things up, and make them look so nice?"

In spite of their best efforts it had proved impossible to do their developing and printing without their handiwork being seen by their companions. The photographs of the school were so good that the girls begged them shamelessly to send home. Gerda was particularly importunate, and even offered to buy copies when they were refused as a gift.

"We don't sell our things," said Dulcie bluntly. "You may go on asking till Doomsday, and you won't get a single print, so there!"

To the chums, Gerda's request was full of significance.

"It shows pretty plainly we're on the right track," said Deirdre. "Of course she wants them to send to her foreign government. They'd pay her handsomely."

"Don't she wish she may get them!" snorted Dulcie.

The affair made an added coolness in their dormitory. Gerda appeared to think them unkind, while they stood more than ever on the alert. They watched her unceasingly. For some days, however, they could find nothing of an incriminating nature in her conduct. Possibly she was aware of their vigilance, and was on her guard against them.

"I believe we're overdoing it," said Deirdre anxiously. "Best slack off a little, and seem as if we're taking no notice of her. Don't follow her about so continually. It's getting too marked altogether. We must be diplomatic."

Just at present Gerda's behaviour was perfectly orthodox. If she went on the warren, it was invariably as one of a "threesome", and the chums could detect her in no more solitary and clandestine excursions. She seemed to have assumed a sudden interest in salvaging, and particularly in the beacon which the girls were beginning to build upon the headland. No one was ready to work harder in carrying up the pieces of driftwood from the beach, and piling them on to the great stack which every day grew a little higher and higher, till it really began to be a conspicuous object, and could be seen from both the villages of Pontperran and Porthmorvan, and from the sea. It was at Gerda's suggestion that a Union Jack, fastened to a pole, was kept flying from the top—a little piece of patriotism which appealed to the school at large, though it roused suspicion in the minds of the chums.

"It's a signal, of course," said Dulcie.

"Some fine day she'll pull it down, and substitute the German flag," agreed Deirdre. "She's only waiting her opportunity."

"Unless we circumvent her. There are two Britishers here who mean to look after their country!"

It was curious how many little things, really quite trivial in themselves, seemed to point in the direction of the chums' fears. Miss Birks greatly encouraged a debating society among her girls, and on her list of subjects for discussion had placed that of "National Truth versus Diplomatic Evasions". Gerda had certainly been chosen to speak for the opposition, and was therefore pledged to the side of diplomacy; but Deirdre and Dulcie thought she made far too good a case of it, and pleaded much too warmly the cause of the ambassador who on behalf of his country's honour is obliged to meet guile with guile, and outwit the enemy by means of stratagems and deeply-laid schemes.

"Any expedient is allowable for the sake of your fatherland," she had contended, and Dulcie quoted the words with a grave shake of her head as she talked the matter over with Deirdre.

"Notice particularly that she said fatherland! Now the Vaterland is always Germany. She didn't mean Britain, you may depend upon it. No —she's planning and scheming for another war!"

"Then we'll plan and scheme for King George! We'll accept her principles, and 'make use of any stratagem to outwit the enemy'."

So they waited and watched, and watched and waited, in what they flattered themselves was true Machiavellian style, till they were almost growing tired of so fruitless an occupation.

Then one day, quite unexpectedly, something happened. It was a wild, windy March morning, and the girls were taking a hasty run on the warren between morning school and dinner, to "blow away cobwebs" and give them an appetite. There was not time to go far, but they dispersed in all directions, trying which could make the biggest distance record available. Gerda had started with Annie Pridwell and Betty Scott, but under pretence of beating their speed she had got considerably ahead and left them panting in the rear.

"Where's Gerda?" asked Deirdre, who, with Dulcie and Evie Bennett, had followed the first "threesome".

"We simply can't keep up with her! She walked as if she had seven-leagued boots. She's gone over the hill there. I'm going to wait till she comes back."

"There's no sense in flying like the wandering Jew!" protested Betty. "I hope she won't be long, because I don't want to walk back as fast as I came."

"Dulcie and I'll go after her," said Deirdre promptly. "We don't mind running. You two can be toddling along with Evie as leisurely as you like."

It only meant a change of "threesomes", so the girls agreed readily and departed at once, leaving the chums to act escort to the truant.

"She's done it on purpose," gasped Dulcie as soon as they were alone.

"Of course. It's a perfectly transparent dodge. Now we must do Secret Service work again and not let her see she's being followed."

The chums really congratulated themselves that they were getting on in the matter of scouting, they availed themselves so cleverly of the cover of rocks and bushes and proceeded with such admirable caution and care. Their efforts were successful, for after a few minutes of skilful stalking they caught sight of their quarry.

Gerda was climbing down the cliff side, fully a hundred feet below them, and had nearly reached the level of the beach. She descended quickly, almost recklessly, scrambling anyhow over rocks and through brambles, and splashing through a boggy piece where a trickle of water had formed a pool. Arrived on the shingle, she went straight to a hole among the rocks, searched in the seaweed, and produced a bottle. Taking a piece of paper from her pocket, she folded it into a long narrow slip and put it inside, replacing the cork tightly. Then she ran towards the crag at the mouth of the cove, and climbing up higher than was compatible with safety she hurled the bottle as far as she could throw it into the sea. She stood looking for a moment or two as it bobbed about on the surface of the water, then, turning round, began to scramble back with more haste than care.

"We've seen enough! Come quick before she spies us!" whispered Deirdre, dragging Dulcie away. "We mustn't let her know we were anywhere near. Let us run and be a long way off before she gets to the top of the cliff and sees us."

The clanging of the first dinner bell, which could plainly be heard in the distance, certainly offered a reasonable excuse for hurry. The chums fled like hares, and even with their best efforts only took their places at table when grace was said and the beef carved. Gerda was later still and scurried in, hot and breathless, after the potatoes had been handed. She drank her whole glassful of water at a gulp. Deirdre and Dulcie avoided looking at her, but they nudged each other secretly. It was a satisfaction to know what she had been doing, though they could not openly proclaim their rejoicing. The penalty for lateness at meals was a fine, but they put their pennies in the charity box with the feeling of philanthropists. They considered them as contributions to a most excellent cause.

It was Wednesday, and a half-holiday. At three o'clock the whole school was to start for a walk to Avonporth, and in the meantime the girls were expected to busy themselves with minor occupations. A certain number were due at the pianos for practising or music lessons, and from the rest stocking-darning, mending, and the tidying of drawers would be required. Gerda marched off with a volume of Beethoven, and was soon hard at work on the Moonlight Sonata under Mademoiselle's tuition. She played well, for she had been carefully taught in Germany, and had a good execution and sympathetic touch.

Deirdre and Dulcie stood outside the door for a moment or two listening to her crisp chords.

"She's boxed up there safe for an hour," commented Deirdre.

"Yes, Mademoiselle won't let her off," agreed Dulcie.

"I could do my darning after tea, and my drawers are as tidy as tidy."

"So are mine!"

"Should we? Do you think we dare?"

"Yes, yes. I'm game if you are."

Then the pair did a scandalous deed, such as they had never even contemplated in all their schooldays before. They took French leave and went out on to the warren. They knew the consequences would be disastrous if they were caught, for they were breaking three rules all at once, absenting themselves without permission, going two together instead of in a "threesome", and being on the headland at a forbidden hour. Perhaps the very riskiness of the undertaking added to its enjoyment.

"We must try and get that bottle, and here's our opportunity," said Deirdre.

"We can't explain to Miss Birks now, but we can tell her some day that we went out of sheer necessity," argued Dulcie.

"Of course; it's only our duty. Even the best of rules have to be broken sometimes when it's a matter of expediency. Miss Birks will quite appreciate that."

"Yes—when she knows the whole."

Meantime Miss Birks did not know, and the sense that their disinterested motives might be liable to misinterpretation caused the chums to proceed

THE SCHOOL BY THE SEA

warily and avoid exposing themselves to any observer from the upper windows. They tacked along bypaths and went rather a roundabout route to reach their destination. Their hope was that the rising water might have washed the bottle back on to the beach, for Gerda's arm had not been strong enough to throw it sufficiently far to carry it into the open sea, and when they last saw it it had been whirling round and round at the mouth of the creek. They climbed down the cliff side by the same track that she had followed, and ran eagerly to the edge of the waves.

The tide was much higher than it had been before dinner, and was rolling up its usual toll of sticks, seaweed, and miscellaneous debris. What was that dark-green object that kept appearing and disappearing, half-hidden by a mass of floating brown bladderwrack? One moment it had vanished, and the next it bobbed up persistently. Deirdre and Dulcie did not wait to ask. With one accord they whisked off shoes and stockings (a proceeding utterly and entirely forbidden except in the months of June and July) and plunged into the water. They were both adepts in the art of salvaging, but no piece of driftwood ever gave them more trouble than that elusive bottle, which dipped and dived and evaded them with the skill of an eel. The beach was shingly, not sandy, which made their fishing not only a slippery but a most agonizing performance. They were obliged to grip each other's hands to keep their foothold at all. At last a larger wave than usual proved helpful, and indeed did its office so thoroughly that it dashed the bottle against Dulcie's shins. With a squeal of pain she caught it, nearly upsetting herself and Deirdre in the process, and the pair hobbled back to where they had left their shoes and stockings.

"Ugh! I'm absolutely lame! I didn't know stones could cut so," complained Deirdre.

"Look at my leg! It will be black and blue, I know," groaned Dulcie.

The possession of the bottle, however, was ample compensation for any scars they might have won in the struggle for its acquisition. They tried with impatient fingers to pull out the cork, but as that proved obdurate they cut the Gordian knot by breaking the neck on a stone. The thin piece of foreign note-paper was quite untouched by wet. Together they unfolded it, knocking their heads in their eagerness to read it both at once. At last, surely, they were within reach of Gerda's secret. But the letter was written in German, and alas! the chums were still in the elementary stages of the language, so that except for a chance word here and there they could not decipher a line of it. Their disappointment was keen.

"What does she mean by writing in her wretched old Deutsch?" demanded Dulcie indignantly.

"Oh, bother her! I wish I could read it!" moaned Deirdre.

Never had the advantages of education appealed to the girls more strongly. They began to think quite seriously of the necessity for studying foreign languages.

"Why didn't I have a Fräulein in my babyhood instead of an ordinary English nursery governess?" lamented Deirdre.

"We may be able to do something with a dictionary," said Dulcie more hopefully.

The idea was consoling enough to prompt them to put on their shoes and stockings, pocket the document, and climb the cliff. After all, if they could make little out of it themselves, they had at least prevented the message from falling into the hands of the person for whom it was destined, and so had frustrated Gerda's intention. That was sufficient reward for their trouble, even without the chance of learning its contents.

"We can keep asking separate words or even sentences until we can piece it all together," said Dulcie sagely.

"Right you are! and now we'd best rush back as fast as we can."

Time waits for nobody, and during their excursion to the beach it had seemed to roll on above the speed limit. Unless they meant to be late for the walk, they must hurry. They were obliged to skirt the cliffs, for they did not dare to show themselves on the open tract of the warren. It was not particularly easy to make haste along a narrow path beset with briers and riddled with rabbit holes. Deirdre went first, because she always naturally took the lead, and Dulcie, whose physical endurance was less, panted after her a bad second. Suddenly Deirdre stopped, and, shading her eyes with her hand, looked intently over the sea at a small object in the far distance.

"What's that?" she asked sharply.

For a moment or two it had the semblance of a huge bird, then a strange whirring noise was heard, and as it drew rapidly nearer and nearer they could see it was an aeroplane flying at no great height over the water. Apparently it was aiming for the exact spot where they were standing, and, quite scared, the girls crouched down beside a gorse bush. With a loud whirr it passed over their heads, and, steering as easily as a hawk, alighted gently on the moorland only about a hundred yards farther on.

Here was a pretty state of things! Had the vanguard of the German army arrived already? And did the enemy mean to swoop down on the school? They peeped timorously from behind the bush and saw two airmen in full oilskins dismount hastily and make an examination of the machine. Whether they were Germans it was impossible to tell; they spoke in tones too low for their words to carry, and certainly their garments gave no hint of their nationality. They looked round searchingly, as if verifying their whereabouts, glanced in the direction of the girls who cowered under their gorse bush, devoutly hoping they were not visible, and consulted a map; then, after an earnest conference, entered their machine again and started off in a northerly direction, flying over the warren towards Avonporth. The chums, almost spellbound, watched the aeroplane till it waned into a mere speck in the sky; then fear lent them wings and they scuttled back to school at a pace they had never attained even at the annual sports. Fortune favoured them, and they managed to dodge unnoticed into the garden, run round to the front, and just in the nick of time take their places among the file of girls assembled on the drive.

Nobody mentioned the aeroplane, so evidently nobody but themselves could have seen it. Whence it came and where it was going remained a mystery, though Deirdre and Dulcie had a settled conviction that Gerda could have enlightened them on that point. She was quite unconscious of the trick they had played her, and as they walked just behind her they chuckled inwardly at the knowledge that her cherished letter lay in Deirdre's pocket. Outward and visible triumph they dared not venture on: it was too dangerous an indulgence for those who wished to keep a secret. As it was, they found it difficult to evade the enquiries of their friends.

"What became of you two just now?" asked Evie Bennett. "Miss Harding was inspecting drawers, and she sent me to fetch you. I'd such a hunt all over the place and couldn't find you anywhere."

"You're a notoriously bad looker, you know, Evie," returned Deirdre, laughing the matter off.

"So Miss Harding said; but it isn't fair to expect one to find people who aren't there."

"Perhaps Betty had mesmerized us into the hypnotic state and rendered us invisible to mortal eyes such as yours!"

"Now, don't rag me! Oh, wasn't that joke spiffing! I shall never forget VA with their faces all streaked with black! I laughed till I nearly died. They haven't forgiven us, and I believe they're plotting something to pay us back in our own coin."

"Let them try, if they like. We're not easily taken in."

"By the by, I was hunting for you two just now," Annie Pridwell broke in. "I wanted to borrow some darning wool, and as I couldn't find you I helped myself off your dressing-table. I don't know whose basket it was I rifled. I took the last skein."

"Mine, but you're welcome," said Dulcie. "My stockings are darned for this week, and shown to Miss Harding and put away. I'll get some more wool on Saturday, if we go to the village."

"But I couldn't find you when I looked for you," persisted Annie.

"Yes, where were you?" asked Evie again.

But to such an inconvenient question the chums prudently turned deaf ears.

Deirdre and Dulcie were determined to leave no stone unturned until they had obtained a translation of the letter which they had purloined from the bottle. They did not care to show the manuscript itself to any of the elder girls, as to do so might be to betray their secret, but by dint of asking odd sentences and words they made it out to run thus: "Very little to report. No progress at all just at present. Extreme caution necessary. Better keep clear of headland for a while, and let all plans stand over." There was neither beginning nor signature, and no date or address.

To the chums the communication had only one meaning. It must refer to a German attack upon the coast. The aeroplane had probably been prospecting for a suitable place to land troops. It was Gerda who was to supply the information needed by the foreign government as to a favourable time for executing a master-stroke.

Evidently she did not consider the hour was yet ripe. For the present England was safe, but who knew for how long?

"It's that man in the brown jersey who's engineering the mischief," said Deirdre. "When we see him sneaking about in his boat we may know there's something on foot."

"What ought we to do?" asked Dulcie doubtfully.

"Nothing can be done just now, if they're on their guard and lying low. We must be vigilant and keep a general eye over things. If anything unexpected crops up we can warn the police. But, of course, we should have to have very good grounds to go upon in that case, a perfectly circumstantial story to tell."

"We've nothing but suspicions at present."

"That's the worst of it. We want more direct evidence. They might only laugh at us for our pains, and we should get into trouble with Miss Birks for interfering in concerns that aren't ours. No; we'll keep the police as the very last resource, and only tell them what we know in the face of a great emergency."

CHAPTER X

Marooned

MISS BIRKS'S birthday fell on the 1st April, and so did Betty Scott's. It was not a particularly happy date for an anniversary, but they both declared they liked it. To Betty it was certainly a chequered event, for the girls treated her to the jokes they dared not play on the head-mistress, and she had to endure a double dose of chaffing. But, on the other hand, a birthday shared with Miss Birks was luck above the common. There was invariably a whole holiday, and some special treat to celebrate the occasion. The nature of the festival depended so entirely upon the day that it was not generally decided till the last minute, which added an element of surprise, and on the whole enhanced the enjoyment. Whether this year's jollification would be outdoors or indoors was naturally a subject of much speculation, but the morning itself settled the question. Such a clear blue sky, such brilliant sunshine, and so calm a sea pointed emphatically to an excursion by water, and Miss Birks at once decided to hire boats, and take the school for a picnic to a little group of islets due west of the headland.

The girls loved being on the sea, and did not often get an opportunity of gratifying their nautical tendencies, for they were, of course, never allowed to hire boats on their own account. Miss Birks was too afraid of accidents to permit lessons in rowing, though many of her pupils thirsted to try their skill with the oars, and had often vainly begged leave to learn in the harbour. To-day three small yachts, with steady and experienced boatmen, were waiting by the quay at Pontperran, and even Mademoiselle—the champion of timorous fears—stepped inside without any nervous dread of going to the bottom of the ocean. It was delightful skimming out over the dancing, shining water, so smooth that the worst sailor could not experience a qualm, yet lapping gently against the bows as if it were trying to leap up and investigate the cargo of fair maidens carried on its bosom. With one accord the girls struck up some boat songs, and the strains of "Row, brothers, row!" or

"Speed, bonny boat, like a bird on the wing, Over the sea to Skye,"

rang clear and sweet in the fresh spring air.

Everybody agreed that the passage was too short, and they were almost sorry when they arrived at their destination. The islands were nothing more than a group of five rocks, too small for cultivation, and inhabited only by sea-birds. Some rough grass and bushes grew on the largest, where there was also a shelving sandy strip of beach that formed a safe landing-place. Here all disembarked, and the provision hampers were carried ashore, together with the big iron trivet and cauldron used for picnics. There was something very fascinating in thus taking possession of a desert island, if only for a few hours. For the present the school felt themselves a band of girl Crusoes, and set to work at once in pioneer fashion to make preparations for lunch. There was an ample supply of drift-wood lying above high-water mark to serve as fuel under their trivet, so while some got the fire going, others took garden spades which they had brought with them and dug sand seats sufficient to accommodate the company. The chairs destined for the mistresses were quite superior erections, provided with backs, and that of Miss Birks was adorned with shells, specially collected from the rocks by a committee of decoration told off for the purpose. In shape and elaboration of ornament it resembled a throne, and as a finishing touch the motto "A Happy Birthday" was placed in yellow periwinkles at the foot.

By the time these extensive preparations were finished, the cauldron was boiling, for the fire had been well kept up, and replenished with wood. Miss Harding dropped in the muslin bag containing the tea, Jessie Macpherson assumed command of the milk can, and a willing army carried cups and laid out provisions. The boatmen were provided each with a steaming pint mug of tea, and a basket of comestibles amongst them, and retired to one of the yachts with grins of satisfaction on their countenances. That hospitality having been settled, the cauldron—which combined the function of urn as well—flowed busily, filling cup after cup till the whole school collected on the sand seats to do justice to the provisions. There were rival birthday cakes: Miss Birks's, a nobly-iced erection decorated with candied violets, was perhaps the larger of the two, but Betty's—sent from home—had the glory of fifteen coloured candles.

"Yours ought to have had candles too, Miss Birks," she said, as she carefully struck a match.

"I'm afraid they'd be too thick on the ground!" laughed Miss Birks. "I used to have them when I was a child, but I barred the exhibition of my years after I was twenty-one."

"I once knew a gentleman who had a huge birthday cake with seventy candles on, and all his grandchildren came to his party," volunteered Hilda Marriott.

"That must have been a truly patriarchal cake, and something to remember. I'm afraid I can only offer you candied violets. Betty, shall we each cut our first slice at the same moment? Here's to everybody's health and prosperity and good luck for the rest of the year!"

It was the first real picnic since last autumn, so, added to the double birthday, it seemed a more than ordinary festivity, and everybody waxed particularly jolly. Miss Birks told humorous Irish stories, and made endless jokes; even Miss Harding, usually the pink of propriety, was guilty of an intentional pun. The merry meal was over at last, and when the baskets had been repacked, all dispersed to wander round the tiny island. It did not differ particularly from the mainland, but the girls found it amusing to investigate new coves, and ramble about on the grassy expanse at the top of the cliffs. A few sought out Miss Birks and begged to be allowed to explore the next largest islet of the group, so after a little discussion half a dozen were sent off under charge of Miss Harding in one of the boats. As there only remained about forty minutes before it would be necessary to go back, it was arranged that this boat should not waste time by returning to the bigger island, but should start on its own account, independently of the other two, as soon as its party had made a brief survey of the islet.

Deirdre and Dulcie, who were venturesome climbers, took advantage of the extra liberty allowed them on this special day to escape by themselves without the tiresome addition of the usual third, and scaled the very highest point of the rocky centre. Here they found they had an excellent view of the whole of the small group, and could command a prospect of cove and inlet quite unattainable from the shore. Dulcie had brought a pair of field-glasses, and with their aid distant objects drew near, and what seemed mere specks to the ordinary vision proved to be sea-birds, preening their wings, or resting upon the rocks. They watched with great interest the progress of the boat to the other island.

"Didn't know Miss Birks was going to let anyone go, or we'd have gone ourselves," lamented Deirdre. "Who's in her? Can you see?"

"Perfectly. Miss Harding and Jessie Macpherson, Phyllis Rowland, Doris Patterson, Rhoda Wilkins, Irene Jordan, and Gerda Thorwaldson. David Essery is rowing them."

"Oh, I wish we'd gone!" repeated Deirdre enviously. "Give me the glasses, and let me take a look."

It was a very long look, that swept all round the islands and took in every detail of cliff and rock. Deirdre repeated it twice, then gave a sudden exclamation.

"Dulcie, you see that big black cliff over there—rather like a seal—count three points farther on, and tell me if you don't think there's a boat in that tiny inlet."

Dulcie seized the glasses, and proceeded to verify the statement.

"It is! Oh, it certainly is! It's moving out now from behind the rock. Somebody's in it, rowing—Deirdre! I do believe——"

"Not him!" shrieked Deirdre ungrammatically, snatching the glasses from her friend. "Oh, it is! I'm perfectly persuaded it is! It's just his figure, and he rows in the same way exactly—the man in the brown jersey!"

"Then Gerda's engineered that expedition to go and meet him. It's as plain as plain!"

Their excitement was intense. It did indeed seem an important discovery, and an added link in their chain of circumstances. Should they stay where they were, and watch the meeting through the field-glasses, or would it be possible to follow the matter up more nearly? They resolved to make a try for the latter. Climbing down as rapidly as they could from their point of vantage, they found Miss Birks, and entreated to be allowed to join the party on the other island.

"John Pengelly would row us over, and we'd catch them up immediately," they pleaded. "Oh, do please let us go!"

Miss Birks was in a birthday frame of mind, and prepared to listen to any fairly-reasonable request.

"There would be quite room for you to go home in David Essery's boat," she acquiesced. "Yes, you may go if you wish. John Pengelly can take you at once. Tell Miss Harding I sent you, and you're to return with her party."

The boatman was good-natured, and apparently did not mind making the extra journey. He grinned at the girls as he pushed off.

"Can't have too much of the sea, missies?" he ventured. "I'll soon pull you over there."

He landed them carefully on the second island, then rowed back to the first landing-place to join his fellow boatman and smoke a pipe till it was time to start. Deirdre and Dulcie knew exactly which way Miss Harding and the girls had gone, and their plain duty was to follow them as rapidly as possible, and report themselves as additions to the party. They did nothing of the sort, however. Instead, they took exactly the opposite direction, and made for the western side of the islet, where they had seen the mysterious boat.

"You may depend upon it we shall find Gerda there," said Deirdre. "It's better not to let her know we're here. We're far more likely to catch her."

With a little scrambling they reached an inlet, which—so they calculated —must be the one they had marked through the field-glasses. They could see no boat, however, and no Gerda. They waited for a while, then rambled farther along the shore, but finding nothing, came back to their former point. They had so entirely counted upon Gerda being there that they felt decidedly disappointed.

"Perhaps she couldn't sneak off," suggested Dulcie. "Miss Harding's very tiresome and particular sometimes."

"I wonder if the boat's waiting about for her?" said Deirdre. "I should very much like to know."

Obeying a sudden impulse, she advanced to the edge of the waves and reproduced, as nearly as she could remember it, the long peculiar curlew cry which Gerda had given as a signal on the former occasion. The effect was instantaneous. There was an answering whistle, and from behind a rock not very far away a small craft shot out into the creek. It was undoubtedly the same white dinghy which they had seen before, and contained the same tall, fair man who had spoken with their school-mate. He rowed forward with a few rapid strokes, then seeing Deirdre and Dulcie he paused, took a searching glance round the shore, turned his boat, and rowed away from the island, passing as quickly as possible behind the shelter of the next of the group. Deirdre stood watching him through the field-glasses as he disappeared. She was not altogether sure whether she had not made a false move. It was perhaps hardly wise to have thus put him on his guard, and let him become aware that they knew of the curlew signal. She already regretted her hasty, thoughtless act. She was conscious that it would defeat her own ends. It seemed no use staying any longer in the creek, for he would certainly not be likely to return after such an alarm.

"We'd better go and find Miss Harding," suggested Dulcie.

It was undoubtedly high time they reported themselves, so, putting the field-glasses back in their case, they set off for the other side of the island. Arrived at the opposite cove, they looked eagerly for their schoolmates, but nobody was to be seen.

"I expect they're a little farther on," suggested Deirdre, hiding the fear she dared not own.

But they were not farther on, and though the girls climbed the cliff, so as to have a thorough view of the shore, and shouted and cooeed till they were hoarse, there was not a sign of a human being anywhere. Far on the horizon were three tiny specks.

Dulcie took out the all-useful glasses, and adjusted the focus anxiously. One glance confirmed her worst apprehensions—the boats had gone, and left them behind! It was perfectly easy to see how it had happened. Miss Birks, having sent them specially across the sound, believed them to be with Miss Harding's party, and Miss Harding did not even know that they had left the larger island. It was their own fault entirely for not reporting themselves. While they had been watching the mysterious boatman on the wrong side of the island, the others must have been starting, utterly unconscious that two of their number were missing.

"We're marooned! That's what it amounts to." Deirdre's voice shook a little as she made the unwelcome admission.

"Well, of all idiots we're the biggest! We have got ourselves into a jolly fix!" exploded Dulcie.

It was highly probable that they would not be missed until the arrival at the harbour. Then, no doubt, someone would come back for them, but the tide was rising rapidly, and perhaps by the time a boat could return it would not be possible to land and take them off. The prospect of a night spent on a desert island was not enlivening. Then, too, came another fear. The mysterious stranger was in the near neighbourhood. Hidden behind rocks and creeks he might have accomplices, who might take it into their heads to reconnoitre. The idea was horrible. They felt an intense dread of the unknown man in the brown jersey. He must be very angry that they had discovered his signal. Suppose he were to find them, and wreak his vengeance upon them? They bitterly rued their folly, though that did not mend matters in the least.

"We won't go over to that side of the island again, in case he might see us," quavered Dulcie. "Let us sit down here, in this sheltered corner. How cold it's getting!"

"I'm hungry, too," sighed Deirdre. "There's nothing to eat on the place except raw periwinkles!"

The sun had set behind a bank of grey clouds, and even in the last ten minutes the daylight had faded noticeably. A chilly wind had sprung up, and the girls shivered as they buttoned their coats closely.

"Do you hear something?" said Dulcie presently.

It was a sound of oars, and both pricked up their ears, half-nervously, half-hopefully. They did not venture to show themselves till they could ascertain whether it were friend or enemy. Hidden under the shadow of the rock, they watched the darkening water, then gripped each other's hands in terror—it was the white boat that appeared round the corner. Its brown-jerseyed occupant was rowing slowly and leisurely, with a careful eye on the shore as he went. Would he see them? They were only partially concealed, and a keen observer might easily detect their presence. To Deirdre those few minutes equalled years of agony—her lively imagination summoned up every possible horror. He paused at last on his oars, and gave the long shrill curlew call. A hundred seagulls screamed in reply. Twice, thrice he repeated it, then apparently judging it a failure, he rowed away in the direction of the mainland.

Dulcie was crying with fright and cold. She let the tears trickle unwiped down her plump cheeks. She was not cut out by nature for a heroine, and would gladly just then have given up all chance of seeing her portrait in the newspapers if she could have found herself safely back in the schoolroom at the Dower House. Adventures might be all very well in their way, but this one had gone decidedly too far.

"I wish you'd never suggested our coming," she said fretfully. "It was your fault, Deirdre."

"Don't be mean, and try and throw the blame on me! You were just as keen as I was!"

"I'm not keen now! I wish to goodness we'd never bothered our heads about Gerda. You won't catch me on such a wild-goose chase again!"

"I'm utterly disgusted with you, Dulcie Wilcox!" returned Deirdre witheringly; and Dulcie wept yet harder, to have added to her physical troubles a quarrel with her chum.

It was almost dark before a search party, consisting of Miss Birks and three boatmen, arrived to fetch them, and the tide had risen so high that it was impossible to land as before, so that John Pengelly had to wade through the water and carry each of them in turn on his back to the boat. Miss Birks said little, but they knew it was the ominous silence before a storm, and that she would have much to say on the morrow. They were intensely thankful when they at last saw the lights of Pontperran, and felt they were within measurable distance of food and fire.

"You provided a nice birthday treat for Miss Birks, I must say," commented Jessie Macpherson sarcastically. "What possessed you to go off on your own in that silly way? There was nothing in the least interesting on that side of the island, and you knew where we were, and that we should be starting almost directly. I simply can't understand such foolishness! Why did you do it?"

But an explanation of the motives that had influenced their conduct was the very last thing in the world that Deirdre and Dulcie felt disposed to offer, even to mitigate the scorn of the head girl.

CHAPTER XI

"Coriolanus"

IT was an old-established custom at the Dower House that at the end of every term the girls must make a special effort to distinguish themselves. They would get up a play, or a concert, or a Shakespeare reading, sometimes a show of paintings, carving, and needlework, or a well-rehearsed exhibition of physical exercises and drill. It was quite an informal affair, only intended for themselves and the mistresses, though occasionally Miss Birks invited a few friends to help to swell the audience. Now April was here, the Easter holidays seemed fast approaching, and preparations were accordingly made for the usual function. As a rule, the girls organized the affair themselves, under the direction of the Sixth Form, but this term Miss Harding stepped in and assumed the management. She decreed that all the members of the Latin classes should give a Latin play, and selected a version of *Coriolanus* for their performance. About half the school took Latin, just enough to make up the cast required, so both senior and junior students were set to work to learn speeches and get up orations. At first they were entirely dismayed at the prospect of so arduous an undertaking.

"I hardly thought Miss Harding was serious when she proposed it," said Annie Pridwell, who with Deirdre, Dulcie, and Gerda made up the four representatives of VB.

"Serious enough in all conscience," groaned Dulcie, turning over the leaves of the small volume with an air of special tragedy. "Volumnia—Volumnia—yes, here she comes again—Volumnia—oh! why am I chosen for Volumnia? I'll never get all this stuff into my head!"

"You'll look the character nicely," said Annie consolingly. "You've really rather a classic sort of nose, and you'll have a big distaff and spindle, and be spinning as you talk."

"That won't help me to remember my part, unless I can write it on a scrap of paper and hide it among the flax. I declare, it's not fair! Volumnia has far more to say than Tullus Attius or Sicinius. You ought to have something extra tagged on to your parts."

"We've quite enough, thanks!" declared Deirdre and Annie hastily.

"As for Gerda," continued Dulcie, "she's being let off too easily altogether. Her Senator's speech is only eight lines."

"Well, it's my first term at Latin, remember," said Gerda.

"Jessie Macpherson will have to swot like anything to get up 'Caius Marcus Coriolanus'. I'm glad I'm not picked for the show part, anyhow."

"Jessie won't mind swotting if she has a chance to shine. There'd have been trouble if she'd had to play second fiddle."

"No one would be rash enough to suggest that. She's not head of the school for nothing."

"Look here! Is this play to be part of the Latin lesson or an extra? Shall we be excused our ordinary prep.?"

"Not a line."

"Oh, what a shame! Then it's giving us double lessons. I wish Miss Harding had left us to get up a concert by ourselves."

Although the girls might grumble and make rather a fuss over learning their parts, they soon committed the little play to memory, and thanks to Miss Harding's efforts rehearsals went briskly. Jessie Macpherson, whose cleverness certainly justified her assumption of general superiority, rose to the occasion nobly, and tripped off her long speeches as if Latin were her mother tongue, to the envy and admiration of those who still halted and stumbled.

"Jessie had got through her grammar before she came to the Dower House, though," said Irene Jordan, herself a beginner. "It gives her an enormous pull to have started early."

"Boys' schools get up ever such grand Latin plays," remarked Rhoda Wilkins. "At Orton College, where my brothers go, they did the *Phormio* of Terence. We went to see it, and it was splendid. It took fully two hours. Ours won't take one."

"Well, one expects boys to be better at Latin."

"Some girls' schools run them hard," said Phyllis Rowland. "I know girls who can beat their brothers."

"Oh, yes, at the big High Schools, where you choose classics or modern languages, and stick to one side. At the Dower House we dabble in everything all round, maths., and science, and accomplishments thrown in as well. Well, it gives you the chance to see which you like best."

The most serious question in connection with the performance was the arrangement of the costumes. Miss Harding and the elder girls pored over illustrated Roman histories and classical dictionaries, trying to get the exact style of the period.

"It's difficult to reproduce with twentieth-century materials," said the mistress. "One feels all the linens ought to be homespun, and woven in a loom like Penelope's; and as for the scenery—well, we shall just have to do the best we can."

"As long as we avoid anachronisms we shall be all right," said Jessie Macpherson. "We shall have to leave something to the imagination of the audience."

The whole school was requisitioned to help, and large working parties were held in the dining-room. The girls found it an amusement to hem togas or construct shields out of cardboard and brown paper, and stitched quite elaborate borders on the robes of Veturia, Volumnia, and Valeria. One of the difficulties that presented itself was the question of footgear. Roman matrons did not wear serviceable school shoes with heels, or elegant French ones either. It would certainly be necessary to contrive sandals.

"We can't cut our best shoes down for the occasion!" said Marcia Richards.

"I'd leave the school first!" returned Phyllis Rowland.

Hiring "Roman" sandals was too great an expense, and an ambitious attempt of Jessie Macpherson's to make them out of paper turned out a ghastly failure.

In the end Miss Harding cut some from strips of cloth, and this effect proved classical enough to serve the purpose.

"That will be the best we can manage," she said.

"I'm thankful I haven't to do a dance in mine. It would be a queer sort of shuffle!" confided Dulcie to her chum.

In honour of the very special effort which was being made, Miss Birks decided to send a number of invitations and ask quite a considerable gathering to an afternoon performance.

"It's going to be really a swell thing for once," said Deirdre. "I hear Miss Birks is getting new curtains—those old ones are quite worn out—and the joiner is to come and fix a rod. And there's to be tea after the entertainment. Such heaps of people are coming!"

"Who?" asked Gerda.

"Oh, Major and Mrs. Hargreaves and their little boys, and Canon Hall and Miss Hall, and Dr. and Mrs. Dawes, and all the four Miss Hirsts, and the Rector of Kergoff, and Mr. Lawson, and of course Mrs. Trevellyan."

"And Ronnie?"

"Rather! We wouldn't leave Ronnie out of it! Miss Herbert is to come too, if she hasn't gone home for the holidays."

"You've never seen Mrs. Trevellyan yet, Gerda?" put in Dulcie.

"Only in church."

"Well, but I mean to speak to. You didn't go to Ronnie's birthday party, and the day she came here you were as shy as a baby, and scooted out of the way."

"I can't help being shy," returned Gerda, blushing up to the very tips of her ears.

"Why, there you are, turning as red as a boiled lobster! Miss Birks says shyness is mostly morbid self-consciousness, and isn't anything to be proud of. Why don't you try to get out of it? It looks right-down silly to colour up like that over simply nothing at all. I'd be ashamed of it!" said Dulcie, who could be severe on other people's faults, though she demanded charity for her own.

"Gerda's copying eighteenth-century heroines!" mocked Deirdre. "They always tried to outvie the rose. Didn't Herrick write a sonnet to his Julia's blushes? And I'm sure I remember reading somewhere:

'O, sweet and fair, Beyond compare, Are Daphne's cheeks. And Daphne's blushing cheeks, I swear!'

Go it, Gerda! Can you possibly get a little redder if you try? If you outvie the rose, there's still the peony left!"

Gerda took her room-mates' teasing, as she took everything else at the Dower House, with little or no remonstrance. It would have pleased the girls much better if they could have raised a spark out of her. Her queer, self-contained reserve was not at all to their taste, and they awarded the palm of popularity to Betty Scott, whose high spirits, perpetual jokes, and amusing tongue made her the public entertainer of the Form.

"I wish Betty were acting," sighed Dulcie. "She's always the life and soul of a play. It was very stupid of her mother not to want her to learn Latin."

"I'm afraid Gerda'll be a perfect stick as Ancus Vinitius," whispered Deirdre.

"An absolute dummy," agreed her chum.

But they underestimated Gerda's talents. Her part was a small one, yet she rendered it excellently. She walked, acted, and spoke with a calm dignity well in keeping with the character she represented. Everybody agreed that she made a most reverend and stately senator.

"I ought to look old, though," she maintained. "It's absurd for us all to look so youthful."

"Powder your hair," suggested Irene.

"Not enough. I think I can do better than that."

Rather to the girls' amusement, Gerda seemed more than ordinarily anxious about her costume.

"She couldn't make more fuss if she was taking Coriolanus himself!" laughed Dulcie. "The Senator might be the chief part."

Gerda had notions of her own, which she proceeded to carry out. She went to Jessie Macpherson and borrowed the white wig, and with the help of some more sheep's wool contrived a beard to match. On the afternoon of the performance she not only donned these, but blackened her eyebrows and painted her face with a series of wrinkles and crows'-feet.

"Why, it's splendid!" exclaimed the girls. "You look seventy at the very least. Just the sort of venerable old city father you're meant for."

"You'd hardly know me, would you?" enquired Gerda casually.

"Nobody would know you. I don't believe even Miss Birks will recognize you. It's the best make-up of anybody's. Jessie'll be proud to see her wig used after all. She'll almost wish she'd worn it herself."

The performers found the dressing nearly the greatest part of the fun. They arranged Volumnia's classical garments and ornaments, adjusted her gold fillet; draped the folds of Veturia's flowing robe, and persuaded Brutus to abandon spectacles for the occasion.

"You forget we're supposed to be in *circum* 490 B.C.," remarked Jessie Macpherson.

"I shall be blind without them!" objected Brutus.

"Never mind! You must catch hold of Sicinius's toga if you get into difficulties."

"The Chinese used spectacles ages ago. Couldn't a pair of them have got imported into Rome?"

"Certainly not. Those goggles of yours would spoil the whole classical spirit of the play, and I shan't allow them."

"Well, I suppose I'll worry through somehow; but if I upset the rostrum don't blame me!"

"You've just got to go through your part without upsetting anything, spectacles or no spectacles, or you'll have to settle with me afterwards!" observed Jessie grimly.

By half-past three all the invited guests had arrived and taken their places in the dining-hall, where a temporary platform had been put up. From behind the curtains the performers could take surreptitious peeps and watch the arrival of the audience. Dulcie, with her eye at a tiny opening, reported progress to the others.

"There's the Vicar! There's Mrs. Hargreaves with all the boys! There's Canon Hall! Oh, here's Mrs. Trevellyan, and Miss Herbert and Ronnie behind her!"

"Where are they sitting?" asked Gerda.

"Right in the middle of the front row. Do you want to peep?"

"Thanks—just for a second. Tell me, is my beard all right? Miss Birks, or—anyone else—wouldn't know me?"

"Not from Adam! What a fuss you make about your costume!" said Dulcie impatiently. "Nobody'll notice it all that much. There are ten others acting as well as yourself."

"I'm glad you snubbed her," said Deirdre, as Gerda having taken her peep between the curtains, retired to the back of the stage.

"She really needs it sometimes. It isn't good for people to let them get swollen head."

"Are you all ready?" asked Miss Harding anxiously. "Then ring the bell, Marcia. Now, Rhoda, don't forget your cue, 'Satis verborum,' and remember to speak up. And, Doris, do put the right accent on 'Dulce et decorum est pro patria mori'. I shall be so ashamed if you get it wrong."

The audience clapped vigorously as the curtains parted and disclosed an atrium with Veturia and Volumnia seated spinning and chatting as Roman matrons may very possibly have chatted in the year 490 B.C. The scene was really pretty, and became impressive when Caius Marcius arrived with his proud news. Jessie Macpherson had an excellent idea of acting, and, as her features were classical, she made an ideal personation of the future Coriolanus, putting just the right amount of aristocratic haughtiness into her demeanour and calm command into her tone of voice. Miss Harding had been nervous about many points, but as the play went on, and scene succeeded scene, she breathed more freely. Every girl was on her mettle to do her best, and things that had dragged even at the dress rehearsal now went briskly. Nobody needed prompting, and nobody forgot her cue; all spoke up audibly, and even the lictor, who had been the most difficult to train, did not turn his back on the audience. Though many of the guests certainly could not understand the dialogue, the plot of the play was so palpable that all could easily follow the story from its interesting opening to the end. Coriolanus died nobly, and fell to the ground with a really heroic disregard of possible bruises; and Veturia commanded the sympathy of the entire room as she shared his fate. The performers received quite an ovation as they stood in a line making their bows.

"Really, Miss Birks, your girls are too clever for anything," remarked Canon Hall. "Their Latin was most excellent."

"The soft pronunciation makes it sound just like Italian," said Mrs. Trevellyan. "They deserve many congratulations."

"Yes, they caught the classical spirit of the thing so well," agreed Mr. Poynter, the vicar.

"Considering that many of them are beginners, I think it is fairly well to their credit, and certainly to Miss Harding's," said Miss Birks. "This is the first Latin play they have attempted. Another time they will do better."

The next part of the function was tea in the drawing-room, to which guests and pupils were alike invited.

"Be quick and change your costumes!" commanded Coriolanus behind the scenes. "Here! somebody please unfasten me at the back! Where are my shoes gone to?"

"Why need we change?" interposed Gerda quickly. "It will take so long, tea'll be over before we're ready. Why can't we go in as we are?"

"Oh, yes, let us keep on our costumes!" agreed Dulcie, who liked being a Roman lady. "Miss Harding, mayn't we have tea in character?"

"Why, I dare say it will amuse the visitors. Yes, run in as you are if you wish. Gerda, wouldn't you like to take off that beard and wash your face? Come here and I'll help you."

"No, thanks! I'd rather keep it on, really."

"I don't know how you'll negotiate any tea!"

"I don't mind."

The eleven performers made quite a sensation as they filed into the drawing-room. All the children among the guests wanted to examine their garments and handle their mock daggers. Ronnie in particular persisted in calling his aunt's attention to every detail.

"I like Jessie and Rhoda and Hilda the best," he declared frankly. "I didn't know Marcia at first. And who do you think that old man is? It's Gerda—Gerda Thorwaldson! Gerda, do let Auntie look at you! Yes, you must come! I'll drag you! Here she is, Auntie!"

"How do you do, my dear? Your make-up seems excellent," said Mrs. Trevellyan kindly, smiling as the senator blushed furiously under his painted wrinkles. "Ronnie, you mustn't be naughty! Don't hold her if she wants to go. What a little tyrant you are!"

"Gerda is such a very shy girl," said Miss Birks, as Ronnie loosed his hold and Ancus Vinitius made his escape. "I always have the greatest difficulty in persuading her to speak to strangers. It amounts to a fault."

"A pardonable failing at her age," returned Mrs. Trevellyan. "She'll outgrow it presently, no doubt. At any rate, it's pleasanter than too great self-assurance, which is generally the reproach cast at young people of the period. It's quite refreshing nowadays to meet a girl who is shy."

CHAPTER XII

In Quarantine

HOWEVER excellent the arrangements of a school, and however happy the girls may be there, the word "holidays" nevertheless holds a magic attraction. Miss Birks's pupils thoroughly appreciated the Dower House, but they would not have been human if they had not rejoiced openly in the immediate prospect of breaking-up day. Already preparations were being made for the general exodus; the gardener was carrying down trunks from the box-room, Miss Harding was checking the linen lists, and the girls were sorting the contents of their drawers and deciding what must be left and what taken home.

"These are going to be extra-special holidays," triumphed Deirdre. "You know, my sister's at school at Madame Mesurier's, near Versailles? Well, Mother and I are to have ten days in Paris, so that we can see Eileen and take her about. Won't it be absolutely ripping? I've never been abroad before, and I'm just living for it. We're to go and see all the sights. Eileen's looking forward to it as much as I am."

"I'm going to stay with my cousins in Hampshire," said Dulcie. "They're mad on horses, so I shall get some riding. They always give me 'Vicky', the sweetest little chestnut cob. She goes like a bird, and yet she's so gentle. When we're not riding we play golf. Their links are gorgeous."

"Where are you going, Gerda?" asked Deirdre.

"To London, to meet Mother," replied Gerda, with a light in her eyes such as the chums had not seen since she arrived. She offered no details of further plans, but evidently the prospect satisfied her. All three girls were counting the hours till their departure. There is a dour old proverb, however, which states that "there's many a slip 'twixt cup and lip", and for once its pessimistic philosophy was justified.

On the very morning of the breaking-up day Deirdre, who had passed a funny, feverish night, woke up to find her face covered with a rash. Dulcie went for Miss Birks, who, after inspecting the invalid and finding on enquiry that both Dulcie and Gerda had slight sore throats, forbade the three to leave their bedroom until they had been seen by a medical man. Very much disconcerted, they took breakfast in bed.

"It may be only nettle-rash," said Deirdre. "I had it once before when I'd eaten something that disagreed with me."

"And I expect Gerda and I caught cold on the warren yesterday. No doubt it's nothing," said Dulcie, trying to thrust away the horrible apprehensions that oppressed her.

When Dr. Jones arrived, however, and examined his patients he sounded the death-knell of their hopes. He pronounced Deirdre to be suffering from a slight attack of German measles, and from Dulcie's and Gerda's symptoms diagnosed that they were sickening for the same complaint.

"The rash will probably be out to-morrow," he announced. "With care in the initial stages it should prove nothing serious, but for the present they are as well in bed."

The three victims could hardly believe the calamity that had overtaken them. To stop in bed with measles when their boxes were packed and the last things ready to go into their hand-bags, and their trains arranged and their relations notified of the time of their arrival!

"It's—it's rotten!" exclaimed Deirdre, turning her flushed face to the wall.

"If it's German measles I believe it's your fault, Gerda!" declared Dulcie, weeping openly.

"I didn't start them!" objected poor Gerda.

"You've had them packed in your box, then!" snapped Dulcie, who was thoroughly cross and unreasonable. "Oh, won't it make a pretty hullaballoo in the school?"

The sympathies of the moment might well be with Miss Birks. She had caused each of her remaining seventeen pupils to be examined by the doctor, and as all appeared free from symptoms was sending off seventeen telegrams to inform parents of the circumstances and ask if they wished their daughters to return home or to remain in quarantine. Without exception the replies were in favour of travelling, so the usual cabs and luggage carts drove up, and the girls, rejoicing greatly, were packed off under Miss Harding's escort by the midday train to Sidcombe Junction, where they would change for their various destinations.

In spite of strict injunctions to keep warm, Deirdre got out of bed and watched the departure from the window.

"To think that I ought to have been sitting inside that bus, and my box ought to have been on that cart!" she lamented. "Oh, I could howl! Mother will have got our tickets for Paris. I wonder if she'll go without me? Oh, why didn't I powder my face and say nothing about it?"

"You couldn't have hidden that rash! Besides, it's horribly dangerous to catch cold on the top of measles. Get back into bed, you silly! I'll tell Miss Birks if you don't! Do you want what the doctor called 'complications'? I think you're the biggest lunatic I know, standing in your night-dress by an open window!" Dulcie's remarks were sage if not complimentary, so Deirdre tore herself away from the tantalizing spectacle of the start below and dutifully returned to her pillow just in time to save herself from being found out of bed by Miss Birks, who, having said good-bye to the travellers, came upstairs to condole with the three invalids.

"I can't think how we caught it!" sighed Dulcie.

"At our performance of *Coriolanus*, I'm afraid," said Miss Birks. "Dr. Jones tells me that all the little Hargreaves are down with it. He was called in to attend them yesterday. Probably they were sickening for it and gave you the infection."

"I hope Ronnie won't have caught it!" gasped Gerda.

"I trust not, indeed. I shan't feel easy till I have sent to the Castle to enquire about him. It certainly is the most unfortunate happening. But Deirdre may be glad she had not started for Paris. There is nothing so miserable or so disastrously expensive as to be laid up in a foreign hotel.

The proprietor would have demanded large compensation for measles, even if he had allowed her to remain in the house. Probably she would have been removed to a fever hospital."

"Not a pleasant way of seeing Paris!" said Deirdre, summoning up a smile.

"You'll have a holiday there another time, I'm sure. And now you must all be brave girls and try to make the best of things. Fortunately, none of you seem likely to be really ill. We'll do what we can to amuse ourselves."

Miss Birks spoke brightly, and her cheery manner hid her own disappointment, though she might justly have indulged in a grumble, for she had been obliged to cancel all her arrangements for a motor tour and stay to attend to her young patients. The responsibility of looking after them and the subsequent disinfecting which must be done would completely spoil her holiday. She was not a woman to think of herself, however, and she put her aspect of the case so entirely aside that the girls never even suspected that her regrets were equal, if not superior to their own.

As the doctor had prophesied, both Dulcie and Gerda developed the rash on the following day. Fortunately, all three girls had the complaint very slightly, and beyond a touch of sore throat and sneezing were not troubled with any very disagreeable symptoms.

"The microbes have only fought a half-hearted battle, and they are retiring worsted," declared Miss Birks; "they're not as savage as scarlet-fever germs."

"Quite tame ones," laughed Dulcie.

"Germs 'made in Germany' aren't likely to be A1," said Deirdre, with a quip at Gerda.

After a day or two in bed, Dr. Jones pronounced his patients convalescent, gave them permission to go downstairs, and held out the promise of a walk on the warren if they continued to improve. Their period of isolation was a fortnight, after which they were to be allowed to go home for the remaining week of the holidays. If it had not been for the thought of what they were missing, they might have congratulated themselves on having an extremely good time. Miss Birks was kindness itself, and allowed every indulgence possible. They were kept well supplied with books, in cheap editions which could be burnt afterwards, and had licence to pursue any hobby which admitted of disinfection. Dr. Jones brought good reports of the Hargreaves children, who were now convalescent. Ronnie had most fortunately not caught any germs, and was away with Mrs. Trevellyan in Herefordshire. Of the seventeen girls who had returned home, Irene Jordan only had developed a slight rash, so that on the whole the school had escaped better than might have been expected.

After the constant society of their class-mates, the three invalids felt the Dower House to be very large and empty and lonely. It was astonishing how different it seemed now the rooms were untenanted. The whole place wore a changed aspect. In ordinary circumstances they hardly ever gave a thought to the ancient associations of the house, but now they constantly remembered that it had been occupied as a convent, and that hundreds of years ago gentle grey-robed figures had flitted up and down those identical stairs and paced those very same passages. It was the code of the school to laugh at superstition, and none of the girls would confess to a dislike to go upstairs alone, but it was remarkable what excuses they found for keeping each other company.

Gerda was the worst off in this respect, for Deirdre and Dulcie, though ready to accommodate each other, did not show her too much consideration, and would often ruthlessly disregard her palpable hints. They kept very much together, and though not openly rude, made her feel most decidedly that she was *de trop*. She never complained, nor offered the least reproach; her manner throughout was exactly the same as it had been since her first arrival, gentle, reserved, and uncommunicative. Sometimes the chums, out of sheer naughtiness, tried to pick a quarrel with her, but she never lost her self-control, and either kept entire silence, or replied so quietly to their gibes that they were rather ashamed of themselves. To Miss Birks Gerda did not open her heart any more than to her room-mates. She appeared grateful for kindness, but the Principal's best efforts could not make her talk, and on the topic of her home and her relations she was dumb. To any questions she would return the most brief and unwilling answers, and seemed reluctant to have the subject mentioned at all. After several vain attempts to win her confidence, Miss Birks gave up trying, and allowed her to go on in her usual self-contained silent fashion—a negative policy not wholly satisfactory.

All three girls made excellent progress, and Dr. Jones very soon gave permission first for a gentle walk round the garden at midday, then for a longer time out-of-doors.

"We've been making invalids of them, though they're not invalids at all," he said jokingly. "They're nothing but three humbugs! Look at their rosy cheeks! And I hear reports of such excessive consumption of chicken broth, and jelly, and other delicacies, I shall have to diet them on porridge and potatoes. I think Miss Birks is too good to you, young ladies. When I was at school I wasn't pampered like this, I assure you, whatever infectious complaints I managed to catch. They used to dose us with Turkey rhubarb, no matter what our ailment; it was a kind of specific against all diseases, and nasty enough to frighten any microbe away."

"May we go home next week?" pleaded Deirdre.

"Girls who catch German measles don't deserve to go home. But I know Miss Birks wants to get rid of you, so I won't be too severe. Yes, I think I may consider you cured, and give you your order of release for next Wednesday."

That evening three very jubilant girls sat in the small schoolroom scribbling their good news.

"This day week we shall be at home," rejoiced Deidre.

"Oh, goody! I am so glad! I can hardly write sense. I hope Mother'll understand it. She's accustomed to my ragtime letters, though."

"Miss Birks is sending post cards about the trains," volunteered Gerda.

"A good thing, too, for I never remember to put the time. Shall I read you what I've said, Deirdre?

"Darling Mummie,

"I'm coming home—oh! isn't it spiffing? Do let us have trifle and sausages for supper, and let Baba stop up for it. I've made her a present, and it's not infectious, because Miss Birks has had it stoved. And it will be ripping to see you all again. I'm so glad I shan't miss Douglas. I hope Jinks is well, but don't let them bring him to the station to meet me, in case he gets on the line. Oh, high cockalorum for next week!

"Heaps and heaps of love from

DULCIE."

"It's a good thing Miss Birks is sending a post card, you silly child," remarked Deirdre crushingly. "You've never told your mother which day you're coming, to say nothing of mentioning a time."

"Oh, haven't I? No more I have. I'll put it in a P.S. I hope Mother won't forget I said trifle and sausages. She always lets me choose my own supper on the day I go home, and we have it all set out in the breakfast-room. Generally we only get biscuits and milk before we go to bed. I think they might let Baba sit up this time. She's nearly six. Oh, bother! My stamps are upstairs. Do come with me, and I'll fetch them. I simply hate going alone."

"You're as big a baby as Baba," returned Deirdre. "No, I can't and won't and shan't go with you. You must pluck up your courage for once. Dear me there's nothing to be afraid of, you scared mouse."

Thus duly squashed by her own chum, Dulcie made no further plea; she only banged the door in reply, and they could hear her footsteps stumping slowly and heavily upstairs. In a few moments, however, she descended with a much swifter motion, and, looking pale and frightened, burst into the schoolroom.

"There's somebody or something inside the barred room," she gasped. "It —whatever it is—it's tapping on the door. I daren't go past."

Both Deirdre and Gerda rose to the rescue, and—three strong—the girls ventured to investigate. With a few pardonable tremors they drew aside the curtains that concealed the door of the mysterious room. There was nothing to be seen or heard, however. The iron bars had not been tampered with, and all was dead silence within.

"Your nerves are jumpy at present, and you'd imagine anything," decided Deirdre.

"I didn't imagine it. I really heard it. I tell you I did. Oh, I say! There it is again!"

Instinctively the girls clung together, for from inside the door certainly came the sound of rapping, not very loud, but quite unmistakable.

"Who's there?" quavered Deirdre valiantly. But there was no reply. "If you want help, speak," she continued.

The three held their breath and listened. Dead silence—that was all, nor was the rapping repeated.

"I've heard it before," whispered Gerda.

"When?"

"Several times. Once just after I came, and again in the middle of the term, and about three weeks ago. It's always the same. A few taps, and then it stops."

"Did any of the other girls hear it?"

"I didn't ask them."

"It's spooky to a degree. What can it be?"

"Oh, do you think there's anybody inside?" whimpered Dulcie.

"Why didn't he answer, if there was?"

"He might be deaf and dumb. Oh, perhaps that's the secret of the room. Is some poor creature shut up there? Oh, it's too horrible!"

"Don't get hysterical!" said Deirdre. "Mrs. Trevellyan wouldn't go shutting up deaf and dumb people! It is very mysterious, though."

"Shall we tell Miss Birks?" suggested Dulcie.

"No, certainly not. She's always fearfully down on us if we get up any scares about the barred room. Don't you remember how cross she was with Annie Pridwell and Betty Scott last term?"

"Do you ever hear any other noises?" asked Gerda.

"No, only what might reasonably be rats or mice."

"Has anyone any notion what's inside?"

"Not the very slightest. I don't believe even Miss Birks knows."

"Well, look here," said Dulcie. "I shall never dare to go down this passage alone again. One of you will simply have to come with me."

"I don't think we'll very much care to go alone ourselves," returned Deirdre.

"You called me a scared mouse!" Dulcie's tone was injured, as if the epithet still rankled.

"Well, we're three scared mice, and it's a case of 'see how they run!'" laughed Deirdre, getting back her self-possession. "We'll go up and down in threesomes for the future."

"You promise? You'll never make me pass here by myself again?"

"Faithfully, on my honour! We'll act police, and protect you against a dozen possible spooks. Do stop squeezing my arm, you've made it quite sore!"

"I don't know how it is, Deirdre, you never take things seriously. I can't see anything to laugh about myself. The whole thing's queer, and uncanny, and mysterious, and I hate mysteries. Why can't Mrs. Trevellyan have the bars taken down and let us look into the room?"

"Ah! Ask me a harder."

"'While I nodded, nearly napping, suddenly there came a tapping, As of someone gently rapping, rapping at my chamber door,'"

quoted Gerda, who was learning "The Raven".

"You're both determined to make fun of it, and it isn't a laughing matter," complained Dulcie. "I haven't got my stamps yet. Come along!"

CHAPTER XIII

The Life-boat Anniversary

ON the following Wednesday three much-disinfected girls took their places in the train, and started off for the short remainder of their holiday.

"I wish we didn't smell so horribly of carbolic!" protested Dulcie. "I'm sure everybody'll think we're coming from a fever hospital, and give us a wide berth."

"All the better if we can keep the carriage to ourselves," chuckled Deirdre. "Those three old ladies were just going to come in, when they turned suspicious and sheered off in a hurry. I feel rather inclined to label myself 'Recovering from Measles'."

"Then you'd come under the Infectious Diseases Act, and be fined for travelling in a public conveyance. Perhaps they'd turn you out, and put you in the guard's van."

"To give him measles? How kind! But I'd travel in a cattle-truck to get home. Only one week of the holidays left! I mean to get the most amazing amount into the time, I assure you."

Deirdre and Dulcie were travelling together to Wexminster, where their ways parted, and Gerda was to go on to Hunstan Junction, where she would be met by a relative. If she was pleased at the prospect, she did not betray much excitement, nor did she vouchsafe any details of what was in store for her. The chums were too busy with their own plans to concern themselves with hers, and jumped out of the train at Wexminster in such a hurry that they almost forgot to bid her good-bye. Rather conscience-stricken, Dulcie remembered just in time, and turned back to the carriage window.

"Good-bye! I hope you'll have as jolly holidays as mine," she called.

"Thank you!" said Gerda, waving her hand, with a wan little smile, as the train began to move. And for the first time since they had known one another, it struck Dulcie that there was something infinitely sad and pathetic about her mysterious school-fellow.

Could she really be a spy? The chums had discussed the question again and again. Her German associations, her intense reserve, and, above all, her incriminating meetings on the shore, seemed highly suspicious. What was the secret that she so persistently concealed? And what the explanation of the letter she had placed in the bottle? For the present the riddle must remain unanswered. Both they and she had turned their backs on Pontperran for one brief week, and during that time neither suspicions nor speculations must disturb the full bliss of their belated holiday.

Deirdre and Dulcie made up for the shortness of the vacation by the thorough enjoyment of each precious day, and when they returned to the Dower House had enough material for conversation to last them a month or more. Even Gerda appeared cheered by the change. Though she did not offer any details of her doings, she admitted she had enjoyed herself in London. She looked brighter, and was more ready than formerly to join in the life of the school and take some part in all that was going on. The chums watched her closely, but found her conduct perfectly regular and orthodox. She indulged in no more surreptitious expeditions to the shore, and did not attempt, when on the warren, to separate herself from the others. Since the day they had been marooned on the island, Deirdre and Dulcie had not seen the brown-jerseyed stranger again. They concluded that he must have left the neighbourhood, and have suspended his evil designs till a more favourable season.

Though they could not in any degree trust her, they certainly found Gerda a more genial companion than she had been last term. Her reserve about her own affairs remained unshaken, but she began to show an interest in school doings. She took keenly to tennis, and improved so rapidly that she was soon one of the best players, and even vanquished Jessie Macpherson in singles—a great triumph for VB.

"She's 'Gerda the Sphinx' still, but she's not quite so bad as she was before," said Dulcie.

The bedroom shared by the three girls had been well disinfected and repapered before their return after the measles. They themselves were regarded rather in the light of heroines by the others.

"You weren't quite clever enough, though," said Betty Scott. "If you'd managed to catch it in term time it would have been a real excitement, and perhaps it would have spread, and we should have had one of the dormitories turned into a nice little hospital."

Betty spoke regretfully, as if she had lost an opportunity which might not occur again. Evidently measles at school was an experience she craved for. Not a solitary germ, however, had survived the stoving and whitewashing, and the health record at the Dower House maintained its former standard of excellence.

The summer term was always of more than usual interest. The school lived largely out-of-doors, many classes were held in the garden, and meals, when weather permitted, were often taken on the lawn. The girls would particularly petition for breakfast in the open air. It was delightful to sit in the warmth of the early morning sunshine, with birds singing in chorus in the trees and shrubs around, and the scent of lilac and hawthorn wafted by the gentle little breeze that was blowing white caps to the waves on the gleaming sea below the cliffs. The whole neighbourhood of Pontperran changed annually after Easter. During the winter it was as sleepy and quiet a spot as could be imagined, with no excitements beyond an occasional temperance meeting or village concert. In the summer it woke up. Every farm or cottage that had a room to spare let it to visitors. The place had a reputation amongst both artists and anglers, and throughout the season easels might be seen pitched at every picturesque corner, and the one hotel blossomed out into the headquarters of the "Izaak Walton Club". So long as the visitors did not attempt to trespass on the headland, the girls rather enjoyed their advent. It was interesting to try to catch a glimpse of an artist's picture as they passed his easel, and the added gaiety in the village found its way to the school. Miss Birks took her pupils to an occasional concert or entertainment, and never omitted to let them attend such important functions as Hospital Saturday Parade and the Life-boat celebrations.

It had been decided by the local authorities this year to keep the Lifeboat anniversary on Whit Monday. On that day large numbers of visitors often came to Pontperran from other seaside places, a circumstance which would largely enhance the possibility of a good collection. The girls at the Dower House, having had a long Easter holiday, were not going home for Whitsuntide, so, with Miss Birks's permission, they were pressed into the service, and requisitioned to sell flowers and take donations. As it was the first time they had been allowed to play such a public part, they were much delighted and excited.

"It's as good as a bazaar, only more fun, because it will be in the streets," said Evie Bennett.

"We'll just make people buy," announced Annie Pridwell. "I'm not going to take a single flower back with me, I've made up my mind about that!"

"I hope people will feel generous," said Elyned Hughes.

It was arranged that the girls should be dressed in white, and should wear their school hats, and a badge consisting of a scarlet sash tied over the shoulder and under one arm. The flowers—imitation corn-flowers—were supplied at the public hall; they were made into tiny buttonholes, which were to be sold for the sum of twopence, or anything more that the charitable felt disposed to give for them. The collectors were to go two and two together, one to sell the flowers, and the other to hold the miniature life-boat into which the pennies were to be dropped. Dulcie begged hard to be allowed to collect with Deirdre, but this Miss Birks would not permit, apportioning an elder girl to each younger one, so that Dulcie, instead of having her chum for a partner, found herself, rather to her chagrin, placed with Jessie Macpherson, the head of the school.

"It isn't going to be fun at all!" she lamented. "I'd almost as soon go about with Miss Harding. I thought we should have had a ripping time. I'll undertake Jessie will want to sell all the flowers herself, and make me rattle the box."

Jessie decidedly had views on the due subordination of younger girls, and would probably have fulfilled Dulcie's gloomy prophecy, had not Miss Birks intervened with the injunction that the seniors were to commence the sale of the flowers, then when half the stock was disposed of, the remainder was to be handed over to the juniors, so that each might have a fair part in the proceedings.

"Jessie looked rather sulky about it," chuckled Dulcie. "I shall see that those flowers are divided equally and she doesn't take more than her legitimate share of them. Twenty buttonholes apiece is the portion. I've a good mind to label mine."

This particular anniversary was to be one of more than ordinary interest, for a new life-boat had been presented to the station, and was to be launched amid general rejoicings. A large influx of visitors was expected, so there seemed every reasonable hope of a speedy sale of the pretty little bouquets.

"I only wish they'd been real flowers," said Deirdre, who, with Irene Jordan, had been apportioned a beat in the main street near the principal shops.

"The real ones fade so horribly quickly," replied Irene. "They would have been drooping by the time we got them down to the town, and they'd only last about an hour in people's buttonholes. These are really very pretty, and can be kept as mementoes. I shan't part with mine till next year. Now, are you ready? I'm going to tackle that old gentleman over there; he looks charitably disposed."

At first the girls were rather shy in pressing their wares, but people responded so kindly and readily that they took courage, and offered them even in unlikely quarters. It was amazing how many and what varied customers they found. A ragged, roguish-looking urchin, who generally begged from them when he could snatch the opportunity, came up now, and invested his twopence in the biggest posy he could select, standing with quite the air of a dandy as Irene pinned the treasure on to his faded little jersey. He dropped the coppers into the life-boat with keen enjoyment, and retired beaming, satisfied that he had contributed his small share to the general fund. Day trippers proved a harvest, some putting threepenny bits or sixpences in place of pennies, and buying more than one bouquet. A waggish young fellow decorated his sailor hat with enough bunches to form a wreath, quite finishing Irene's stock, and encroaching on Deirdre's half of the tray. Several ladies tied bouquets on to the collars of their pet dogs, and a sweet little girl insisted upon making a purchase on behalf of her doll. A small, very spoilt boy wanted to carry off the miniature life-boat, and howled lustily when he realized that it was not for sale; but was consoled when Irene allowed him to hold it for a few minutes, and rattle it suggestively at passers-by. So delighted was he with the novel occupation that his nurse could scarcely tear him away, and it was only by the bribe of a bun that she cajoled him into restoring the box to its lawful owner.

"It's getting almost too full to shake!" laughed Irene. "If everyone else has done as well as ourselves, this ought to be a record day. Oh, look! There's Miss Herbert with Ronnie! They're coming this way!"

"Ronnie must have one of my bunches, if I buy it myself and give it him!" declared Deirdre.

But Ronnie had come with his small pockets well lined with pennies which he was burning to spend. He gallantly chose a buttonhole for his governess first then one for himself, and would have added a third for his aunt had not Miss Herbert reminded him that he would meet other friends with trays of flowers if they walked farther down the street.

"I want to buy some from Jessie," he sighed, "and from Gerda. I do like Gerda—the best of anybody!"

"He's taken quite a fancy to Gerda," laughed Miss Herbert. "He often talks about her. And really she's very kind. She gives him so many picture post cards—the sort he loves, with photographs of animals on them. I think she must get them from Germany. I've never seen any like them in England."

"Gerda's ripping!" remarked Ronnie as he trotted away.

Deirdre looked after him in much astonishment. She remembered how on the occasion of Ronnie's birthday Gerda had paid him a surreptitious visit, and given him a present on her own account, but she had no idea that the friendship had been continued. Gerda must surely have seen him on other occasions, and won his favour. Ronnie was so entirely the "King of the Castle" to the school at the Dower House that Deirdre felt hugely indignant at the notion of her room-mate stealing a march on his affections. It was an extraordinary thing, she reflected, that Ronnie should care for anybody so silent and uninteresting. Then a mental vision returned to her of Gerda's eager, animated face, as she had seen it when she had peeped unobserved over the wall. No, Gerda had not looked silent and uninterested when she was alone with Ronnie.

"The girl's a riddle. I can make nothing of her," decided Deirdre.

By half-past eleven the enthusiastic flower vendors had the extreme satisfaction of finding their trays cleared, and their miniature life-boats grown extremely heavy. They carried the latter to the public hall, and delivered them safely to the secretary of the fund; then, being off duty, they wended their way to the quay to await that most-important function, the launching of the new life-boat. Quite a crowd was assembled, of both visitors and townspeople, and the place for once seemed full almost to overflowing. A long jetty stretched out from the harbour, and here, during the summer months, large numbers of lasses were busy every day packing fish into barrels and boxes. They were a bonny, picturesque crew, most of them wearing gay-coloured handkerchiefs tied over their heads, and short sleeves which showed their well-shaped arms to advantage. They were brought to Cornwall for the summer from Scotland, in a special vessel chartered for the purpose, and performed their task of fish packing with a skill and dispatch in which nobody could rival them.

For the moment they had ceased work, and, wiping the scales from their hands, stood watching the preparations with as keen interest as anybody.

"They're talking Gaelic to each other!" exclaimed Ronnie, running up to Deirdre in great excitement. "Oh, it sounds so funny! Miss Herbert says it's rather like Welsh. I asked one of them to say something, and she just gabbled gibberish, and said it meant I was a sweet, nice little boy. She let me stand on a barrel, and I could see so well, but Miss Herbert made me get down, because she said it was too fishy."

"Come and stand here with me," suggested Deirdre persuasively.

"No, I'm going to Gerda—she's over there and smiling at me. Good-bye!" and Ronnie rushed away tumultuously to join his latest favourite, placing himself so extremely near to the edge of the quay as to have involved imminent danger, had not Gerda held one of his small hands, and Miss Herbert the other.

As everybody seemed to be collected, and the appointed hour of noon was already past, a flag was waved as a signal for the proceedings to begin. First a blank charge was fired, which rang over the water with a tremendous report, scaring those who were not quite prepared for it, and making some people clap their hands over their ears. Then the great doors of the National station swung open, and the beautiful new life-boat came gliding gently out on her path to the sea. All her crew were in new jerseys and scarlet caps, and as the bow of their vessel first touched the water, they broke into a mighty ringing cheer. It was taken up by the crowd, and from every side came hurrahs and shouts of congratulation. Ronnie was flourishing his hat frantically (with Miss Herbert and Gerda both clutching him in the rear) and hurrahing with all the power of his young lungs; the fish packers were clapping and waving handkerchiefs; and even the sea-birds, frightened probably by the gun, screamed as if adding their quota to the general disturbance.

"I do like anything that makes a noise!" declared Ronnie, when the excitement had calmed down a little, and everyone was tired of shouting. "I'm going to ask Auntie to let me fire the two old cannon on the terrace at home when I go back."

"I'm quite sure she won't!" laughed Miss Herbert.

The life-boat made a short trial trip round the harbour, then, returning to the quay, the coxswain announced that they would be pleased to take visitors on board in relays, and gave a special first invitation to the young ladies who had so kindly sold flowers in the interest of the institution.

With Miss Birks's permission the delighted girls descended the stone steps, and were jumped by sturdy sailors into the boat. Ronnie begged so hard to be of the party that his pretty wistful little face gained the day, and the coxswain himself took him in his arms, and handed him safely on board. Very proud he was of his trip, and very loath to go back to dry land when the vessel, after a partial tour of the harbour, returned to take a fresh cargo of young people.

When those of the juveniles among the crowd who cared to venture had had their turn, the crew provided a fresh sensation by giving an exhibition of life-saving. One of their number jumped into the water, and, throwing up his hands, shouted as if in the utmost jeopardy of his life. Immediately the boat was turned, a rope flung, and in record time he was rescued, hauled on board, and revived. The rocket apparatus was next fixed, and the crowd watched with deepest interest as a rope was fired over the vessel, and skilfully caught and attached by the crew, who then drew up the "cradle", a rough canvas bag, in which the passage from the life-boat to the shore must be made. Without wasting a moment one of the men was popped in, then those on shore hauled him as rapidly as possible to land. He kept dipping in the water as he came, so the girls decided that in a real storm it must be an extremely perilous passage, and he would be likely to arrive half-drowned.

"I don't think I'd ever dare to be saved in a dreadful thing like that!" shuddered Dulcie. "I'd rather stay on board and take my chance."

"I wish they'd let me go in it!" said Ronnie. "Are they going to take visitors as passengers? I'm going to run down the steps, and ask them to have me first!"

"No, you're not!" laughed Miss Herbert. "You're getting too obstreperous, young man, and I must take you home. Say good-bye to the girls."

"Good-bye! Oh, hasn't it been glorious! I have so enjoyed myself! When will the next fun be?"

"Not till Empire Day. Then we'll have the beacon fire on the headland."

"Oh, lovely! I wish it was to-morrow! What, Gerda?" as his friend bent over him and murmured something. "Really? Oh, how spiffing! Rather!"

"What was Gerda whispering to you?" asked Deirdre jealously.

"Shan't tell you! It's a secret between her and me," chirruped Ronnie as he danced away.

CHAPTER XIV

The Beacon Fire

THE girls at the Dower House were extremely keen upon celebrating, with due ceremony, every festival that was marked in the calendar. They bobbed for apples on All-Hallows Eve, made toffee and let off fireworks on 5th November, tried to revive St. Valentine's fete on 14th February, practised the usual jokes on 1st April, and plaited garlands of flowers on May Day. They had thoroughly enjoyed Life-boat Monday, and now turned their attention to providing adequate rejoicings on Empire Day. All through the winter they had been collecting drift-wood on the beach, and carrying it to the headland to form the huge bonfire which they intended should be a beacon for the neighbourhood. They had built up their pile with skill and science, and, thanks to their heroic exertions, it had reached quite large and important proportions. A kindly wind had dried the wood, so that there was every prospect of its burning well, and Mrs. Trevellyan had promised a large can of paraffin, to be poured on at the last moment before lighting, so as to ensure a blaze. The only flaw in the arrangement was the fact that the sun did not set until past eight o'clock, and that owing to the long twilight it would probably not be really dark until ten, so that the effect of their beacon would be slightly marred.

"If we could have had it at midnight!" sighed Annie Pridwell.

"Yes, that would have been scrumptious, if we could have got people to come. Ronnie wouldn't have been allowed."

"No; Mrs. Trevellyan's making a great concession as it is to let him stop up till nine. It's a pity she's laid up with sciatica, and can't come herself."

"She'll watch it from a window, and Miss Herbert will bring Ronnie."

Mrs. Trevellyan had been extremely kind in the matter of the bonfire; she had given Miss Birks carte blanche in respect to it, and told her to regard the headland as her private property for the evening, and ask any guests whom she wished to join in the celebration. Quite a number of invitations had been sent out to various friends in the neighbourhood, and a merry gathering was expected. Some were to arrive at the school and walk over the warren, and others had decided to come by boat to the little cove directly under the headland, an easier means of getting from Porthmorvan or St. Gonstan's than going round by road.

Naturally, the girls were all at the very tiptop of expectation: even the dignified Sixth betrayed signs of excitement, and VB was in a state verging on the riotous. To their credit they all accomplished their shortened evening preparation with exemplary quiet and diligence, but once released, and speeding over the warren to the headland, they allowed their overwrought spirits to find relief. They danced ragtimes, sang, halloed, and cooeed, and generally worked off steam, so that by the time they reached the beacon they had calmed down sufficiently to satisfy Miss Birks's standard of holiday behaviour, and not make an exhibition of themselves before visitors.

Already people were beginning to arrive both by land and sea. Miss Birks brought a select party who had motored from Kergoff, and at least half a dozen boats were beached upon the little cove. Ronnie was already on the scene in charge of Miss Herbert, immensely proud of being allowed to sit up beyond his usual bedtime, and running here, there, and everywhere in the exuberance of his supreme satisfaction.

The girls had fixed a stake into the rocks close by, from which a Union Jack floated to give the key-note of the proceedings, and had prepared buttonholes of daisies, the Empire flower, to present to all the guests. They had twisted daisy-chains round their own hats, and even decorated their flagstaff with a long garland, so they felt that they had done everything possible to manifest their loyalty to King George. Mrs. Trevellyan's head gardener had brought the large can of paraffin, and filling a greenhouse syringe from it, began carefully to spray the wood, especially in the places where it was most important for the fire to catch. The company then drew back, and formed a circle at a safe and respectful distance. A thin train of gunpowder was laid down, and under the gardener's careful superintendence Ronnie was allowed the immense privilege of applying a taper to the end. The light flared up, and wound like a fiery snake to the beacon, where, catching a piece of gorse soaked with paraffin, it started the whole pile into a glorious blaze. Up and up soared the flames, roaring and crackling, and making as much ado as if the Spanish armada had been sighted again and it were warning the neighbourhood to arms. The girls could not help starting three cheers, the guests joined lustily, and Ronnie, almost beside himself with excitement, pranced about like a small high-priest officiating at some heathen ceremonial rite.

Miss Birks had added a delightful feature to the celebration by providing a picnic supper. It was of course impossible to hang kettles on the beacon, but the large cauldron had been brought, and was soon at work boiling water to make coffee and cocoa. The girls helped to unpack hampers of cups and saucers, and to arrange baskets of cakes, and when the bonfire had formed a sufficient deposit of hot ashes, rows of potatoes were placed round it to cook, and to be eaten later. It was a very merry supper, as they sat on the short grass of the headland, with the beacon blazing on one hand, and on the other the western sky all glorious with the copper afterglow of sunset. The new moon, like a good omen, shone over the sea, and from far, far away came the distant chime of bells, stealing almost like elfin music over the water. From the beach below came the long-drawn, monotonous cry of a curlew.

"The fairies are calling!" whispered Gerda to Ronnie. "Listen! This is just the time for their dancing—the new moon and the sunset. They'll be whirling round and round and round in the creek over there."

"Really? Oh, Gerda! could we truly, truly see them?"

The little fellow's blue eyes were wide with eagerness. He sprang on his friend's knee, and clutched her tightly round the neck.

"You promised you'd take me!" he breathed in her ear.

"Yes, if you're very quiet, and don't tell. Not a living soul must know but you and me. If anyone else sees us the fairies will all just vanish away. They can't bear mortals to know their secrets."

"But they'll let you and me?"

"Yes, you shall see the Queen of the Fairies, and she'll give you a kiss."

"Oh, do let us go, quick!"

"In a moment. Remember, nobody must notice. Let us walk over there, and pretend we're looking at the flag. Now, come gently round this rock.

Hush! We must steal away if we're to find fairies! I believe we're out of sight now. Not a soul can see us. Give me your hand, darling, and we'll run."

It was perhaps a few minutes after this that Miss Herbert, who had been engaged in a pleasant conversation with the curate from Kergoff, missed her small charge.

"Where's Ronnie?" she asked anxiously.

"I saw him just now," said Miss Harding. "He was with the girls as usual. Gerda Thorwaldson had him in tow."

"If he's with Gerda he's all right," returned Miss Herbert, evidently relieved. "She's always so very careful. No doubt they'll turn up directly."

"I expect they're only fetching more potatoes from the hamper," said the curate. "We'll soon hunt them up if they don't put in an appearance."

Deirdre, who was standing near, chanced to overhear these remarks, and, jealous of Gerda's hold over Ronnie, turned in search of the missing pair. They were not by the bonfire, it was certain, nor were they among any of the groups of girls and guests who still sat finishing cups of coffee, and laughing and chatting. Deirdre walked to where the hamper of potatoes had been left, but her quest was still unrewarded. She returned hastily, and calling her chum, drew her aside.

"Gerda and Ronnie have disappeared," she explained briefly. "I don't like the look of it. Gerda has no right to monopolize him as she does. I vote we go straight and find them, and bring them back."

The two girls set out at once, and as luck would have it, turned their steps exactly in the direction where the truants had gone. They ran down the steep hillside behind the flagstaff, till they reached a broad terrace on the verge of the cliff overhanging the cove where the boats were moored. Ronnie was so fond of boats that they thought he had perhaps persuaded Gerda to take him to the beach to look at them.

Advancing as near to the edge as they dared, they peeped over on to the sands. There was nobody to be seen, only the row of small craft lying on the shingle, just as they had seen them an hour ago. The tide had risen higher, and had begun to lap softly against them, but was not yet sufficiently full to float them; moreover they were all secured with stout cables. Stop! There was something different. Surely there had only been six boats before, and now there was a seventh added to the number—a seventh in whose shadow lurked the dark figure of a man. Suddenly from the beach below rang out Ronnie's clear, rippling laugh, followed by an instant warning "Sh! sh!" and immediately he and Gerda stepped from the shadow of the cliff on to the shingle. They ran hand in hand towards the seventh boat, and the boatman, without waiting a moment, jumped them in, one after the other, pushed off, sprang into his seat, and began to row rapidly away across the creek.

"Look! Look!" gasped Deirdre in an agony of horror. "It's the man in the brown jersey!"

Of his identity they were certain. Even in the failing light they could not be mistaken. And he was kidnapping Ronnie under the very eyes of his friends—Ronnie, the "King of the Castle", the idol of the school, and the one treasure of Mrs. Trevellyan's old age! Where were they taking him? Was he to be held for ransom? Or kept in prison somewhere as a hostage? Gerda, with her smooth, insinuating ways, had betrayed him, and led him away to his fate.

"We must save him!" gasped Deirdre. "Save him before it is too late! Quick, quick! Let us run down to the shore. We mustn't let them get out of our sight."

The two girls tore frantically down the path which led to the sea in such haste that they had not time to realize their own risk of slipping. That Ronnie was being kidnapped was the one idea of paramount importance. As they reached the belt of shingle the dinghy had already crossed the creek, and was heading round the corner of the cliffs to the west.

"What can we do?" moaned Dulcie, wringing her hands in an agony of despair. "Shall we go and call Miss Birks, and get somebody to follow them with a boat?"

"By the time we'd fetched anybody they'd be hopelessly out of sight, and gone—goodness knows where. No! If Ronnie's to be saved, we must act at once, and follow them ourselves. You can row, can't you?"

"Yes, I learnt last holidays at home on the river."

"So can I. Then come, let's choose the lightest boat we can find. We mustn't waste a minute. We're both strong, and ought to be able to manage."

After a hasty review they selected a small skiff as looking the most likely to respond to amateur seamanship, and loosing the cable, which had been secured round a rock, coiled it and placed it inside. The tide had risen so fast that it did not require any very great effort to push off the boat.

"Are you ready?" said Deirdre. "Don't mind getting your feet wet; it can't be helped. Now, then! Heave, oh! She's off!"

With a simultaneous splash the two girls scrambled on board in the very nick of time, and, taking their places, gingerly unshipped the oars. They were neither of them skilled for their task, and both realized that it was rather a wild and risky proceeding. For Ronnie's sake, however, they would have ventured far more, so they mutually hid their feelings, and pretended it was quite an everyday, easy kind of performance. If they had not much experience, their zeal and their strong young arms made the light little skiff fly like a sea-swallow, and they had soon gained the headland round which the other boat had disappeared. Very cautiously they proceeded, for fear of currents, but they managed successfully to pilot their craft past a group of half-sunken rocks and take her round the corner into the next bay. In front through the gathering darkness they could just distinguish the object of their pursuit making a landing upon the opposite shore. They could hear the grating of the keel on the shingle and an excited exclamation from Ronnie. They strained their eyes to watch what was happening. The man in the jersey helped Gerda to land, then taking Ronnie on his back strode rapidly away with him, Gerda walking close by his side. In another moment they had disappeared behind a group of rocks.

If the girls rowed fast before, they now redoubled their efforts. Both were flushed and panting, but they struggled valiantly on, and succeeded in beaching their skiff within a few yards of the white dinghy. They did not wait to cable her, but, anxious not to lose a moment of valuable time, made off in quest of the fugitives. At the other side of the group of rocks it was lighter, for they faced the west, and caught the last departing glories of the sunset. On the sands, bathed in the golden dying gleam of the afterglow, a lady was kneeling and clasping little Ronnie tightly in her arms. Even from the distance where they stood the chums could see

THE SCHOOL BY THE SEA

how very fair and pretty she was. Her hat had fallen on the beach, and her flaxen head was pressed closely against the child's short curls.

"Why, she's actually kissing him!" exclaimed Dulcie.

The scene was so utterly unanticipated, and so entirely different from what they had expected to find, that the two girls stood for a moment almost at a loss. At that instant Gerda spied them, and turning to her companions made some remark in a low tone. The lady immediately loosed Ronnie and rose to her feet. Seeing their presence was discovered, the chums judged it best to walk boldly forward. They had come to rescue Ronnie, and it seemed high time to interfere.

"Miss Herbert's looking for you! You must go back with us at once," said Dulcie, laying an appropriating hand on the child's shoulder and glaring defiance at his kidnappers.

Gerda had blushed crimson. She looked egregiously caught. She glanced at the faces of her fellow conspirators as if seeking advice. The man in the brown jersey nodded.

"Yes—we'll go back at once," she stammered. "I—I was only trying to give Ronnie some fun."

"Miss Herbert doesn't think it fun," said Dulcie grimly. "You'd no business to take him away!"

The chums each seized the little boy by a hand and began to hurry him along towards the boats.

"But where are the fairies? Gerda promised I should see the fairies!" he objected.

"The fairies can't dance now, dear," replied Gerda sadly. "You remember I said they could only come if nobody was watching."

In silence the whole party returned to the shingle bank. Deirdre and Dulcie were too indignant for words, and Gerda seemed overwhelmed with embarrassment. The fair-haired lady was crying quietly. Still, keeping a tight hold on Ronnie, the chums approached their skiff. Then for the first time the man in the brown jersey spoke.

"You'd better all come into my boat," he remarked briefly. "I'll fasten yours on to the stern and tow her along."

The chums started with surprise. Instead of the local dialect of a fisherman or, as they expected, the foreign accent of a German, he had the cultured, refined tone of an English gentleman. For a moment they hesitated. Did he mean to kidnap them as well as Ronnie? Perhaps he saw the doubt in their eyes.

"You needn't be afraid. I'll take you straight back," he urged.

Glad to escape the risky task of rowing round the point and steering clear of dangerous currents, the girls consented, though rather under protest, and wondering at the novelty of the situation which had made them, the pursuers, return in charge of the stranger whom they still distrusted. They sat in the stern, with Ronnie between them, guarding him like two faithful bulldogs. The lady stood upon the shore watching them as the boat pushed off. There was a sad, wistful look in her eyes. She did not attempt to say good-bye.

The chums felt considerably relieved when at last they arrived at the cove again in safety. The man in the brown jersey helped them all to land without a word; then he unloosed the skiff, beached her on the shingle whence she had been taken, and rowed out alone into the bay. Ronnie was growing sleepy; it took all Deirdre's and Dulcie's efforts to help him up the steep cliffside. Gerda followed a short way behind. Miss Herbert, who had really been uneasy about her charge, hailed their arrival with relief.

"Here you are at last! Where have you been, Ronnie? To see fairies! Gerda mustn't tell you such nonsense. Wake up! We must be going home at once. It's after nine o'clock."

The bonfire had burnt low, and the girls were packing the cups into baskets, ready to be carried to the Dower House.

"We ought to tell Miss Birks about this," whispered Dulcie, and Deirdre agreed with her.

Late as it was when they got in, the two girls sought the Principal in her study and poured out the whole of the story—their alarm on Ronnie's behalf, their dread of the man in the brown jersey, and their suspicion that Gerda was a German spy plotting against the country. Miss Birks listened most attentively, putting in a question here and there.

"I don't think either England or Ronnie is in any immediate danger," she said. "You may make your minds easy on that respect. I shall have a word with Gerda presently. You have done right to tell me; but now you may leave the whole matter safely in my hands, and need not worry yourselves any more over it. On no account talk about it to anybody in the school, and unless Gerda refers to it herself, do not mention the subject to her."

"Trust Gerda not to speak of it," said Dulcie as they went upstairs. "The Sphinx isn't likely to offer to unravel the mystery."

"It's a jig-saw puzzle I can't fit together," replied Deirdre. "It's all in odd pieces. Why was that lady crying? And what have she and the man in the brown jersey got to do with Ronnie?"

CHAPTER XV

The Old Windlass

BY this time the reader will probably have gathered that Master Ronald Trevellyan, though possessed of a very charming and winsome personality, had a decidedly strong will of his own. On the whole he was fairly good, but the lack of companions of his own age, and the fact that he was the one darling of the household, made it almost an impossibility to prevent him from becoming in some slight degree spoilt. Mrs. Trevellyan did her best to enforce obedience, but though her word was law, Ronnie was not always so ready to accept the authority of others, and occasionally exhibited a burst of independence. This was particularly noticeable with his governess. Miss Herbert was inclined to be easy-going and was not sufficiently firm with him, and the young scamp, finding he could get his own way, took advantage of her failing and sometimes defied her with impunity. The little fellow's simple lessons were over in the morning, and in the afternoon he either played in the garden or was taken for a walk. To him it was a great occasion if he chanced to meet the pupils from the Dower House. He counted them all as friends, and though he had his particular favourites among them, he was quite ready to be the general pet of the school. On the day but one after the bonfire, when on his way to the beach escorted by Miss Herbert, he encountered the twenty girls walking with Miss Harding towards the headland.

"Hallo, Ronnie boy! Where are you off to? We're all going to drill on the green and do ambulance practice. Won't Miss Herbert let you come and watch us?"

"Not to-day, thanks, I'm busy. I've got to go fishing," returned the "King of the Castle", proudly displaying a small shrimping net. "Auntie's going to have what I catch fried for breakfast to-morrow."

"Hope she won't starve!"

"Hadn't you better run after a rabbit and catch it for her?"

"Or shoot a cock sparrow?"

"Come with us to drill and we'll make you a colonel of the regiment."

"Or we'll practise ambulance work, and bind up your leg and carry you home on a coat."

"You've no idea what fun it would be."

But Ronnie stuck to his guns. He had come out with the intention of fishing, and not even the attractions of drill and ambulance could tempt him from trying his new shrimping net.

"We shall expect a pilchard apiece," declared his friends, as they gave up trying to cajole him and went on their way.

"You won't get any; they're all for Auntie!" he shouted. "Yes, they are, even if I catch shoals, and shoals, and shoals!"

The girls laughed, talked about him for a moment or two, and then dismissed him from their minds. They were full of their practice for the afternoon. It was only this term that drill and ambulance had been taken up at the school, so they were still in the first heat of their enthusiasm. On this occasion, too, Miss Barlow, a lady staying in the neighbourhood, who had been largely connected with the Girl Guide movement in Australia, had promised to come and inspect them and give them some of the results of her Colonial experience. A strip of green sward not far from the scene of the beacon fire made an excellent parade ground, and here they drew up in line to await the arrival of their honorary colonel, who was following with Miss Birks. Miss Barlow proved to be, like an old-fashioned children's book, "a combination of amusement and instruction". She had extremely jolly, pleasant manners and a fund of lively remarks, making everybody laugh heartily as she went her round of inspection.

"I'm glad you know the difference between left and right," she said. "I'm told that country recruits for the army find such a difficulty in distinguishing between the two that their sergeant is sometimes obliged to make them tie a band of hay round one leg and a band of straw round the other. Then instead of calling out 'left—right—left—right' he says 'hay—straw—hay—straw' until they have grown accustomed to march."

"Do you find Colonial girls much quicker than English?" asked Jessie Macpherson.

"They are more resourceful, and very bright in suggesting fresh ideas, but they are not so willing to submit to discipline. They are more ready to copy a corps of roughriders than a Roman cohort. No doubt it is owing to the way they are brought up. Very few of them spend their early life in the charge of nurses and governesses. From babyhood they are taught to take care of themselves, to be prepared for emergencies, and to throw up whatever they may have in hand and go to the assistance of a neighbour who needs them. It is a training that makes them helpful and energetic, but perhaps a little too independent to accord entirely with the standards we keep at home. Our girls are more sheltered and guarded, and it is only natural that they should have a different style from those who must hold their own. I wish I could have introduced you to some of my bright young Australian friends. I think you would find the same charm about them that I do."

Miss Barlow had many hints to give them on the subject of camp cookery. She showed the girls the quickest and most practical way to build a fire, and the right situation to choose for it as regards shelter.

"I wish we could have stayed here for a whole day and prepared our own dinner," she said. "It is wonderful how much can be done with a three-legged iron pot and some gorse to burn under it. We would have made a most delicious stew. I should have liked to teach you to build a camp oven, but we should need a spade for that. One has to dig a hole nearly a yard deep and wide, line it with stones, light a fire in it, then pop one's iron pot on to the mass of hot ashes, and cover the whole with a roof of sticks and sods. I have often baked bread this way out in the bush. Then you ought to know how to wrap up your food in cases of green leaves and wet clay, to be cooked in the ashes round an ordinary camp fire; and how to mix flour and water cakes when there is no yeast to be had for bread."

"If only we could come and camp out with you here for a week!" sighed the girls. "It would be ripping fun!"

"Yes, if the weather were fine; but our English weather is apt to play unkind tricks. My brother is a doctor, and medical officer to a Boys' Brigade. At Whitsuntide he went with them to camp. It was delightful for the first three days, then in the night a perfect blizzard arose and the rain fell in torrents. The wind got under his tent and tore up some of the pegs, then half the canvas came flapping down, a wet mass, over his bed. A tightly-stretched tent will keep out the weather, but if it gets loose and rests against anything inside, the rain will soak through, and you can imagine the miserable condition. In preparing breakfast, &c., all the boys got wretchedly wet, and to try to prevent their taking cold my brother dosed them all with camphor. As there were eighty in camp, you can understand it took a long time to measure out the orthodox ten drops on to each separate lump of sugar. I am afraid the last patient had full opportunity of catching the cold before he took the cure."

"I expect the ancient Britons did camp cookery when they lived here," suggested Irene Jordan.

"No doubt they did. There are traces that a most early and primitive people, far older than the Celts whom Julius Cæsar wrote about, must have lived on this headland. We are sitting on the very remains of their little circular huts. Look! you can trace the outlines of the ancient stone walls. Here a small community must have lived, and hunted and fished, and fetched limpets and periwinkles from the beach to eat as dessert. Probably the reindeer or the Irish elk still came to feed on the mossy grass, and there would be a grand pursuit with bows and flint-tipped arrows. It must have been a great event to kill an elk. The whole primitive village would feast for days afterwards, toasting the flesh on little spits of wood. Then the women would prepare the skin and stitch it with bone needles into warm garments, and the horns would be used as picks or other implements, so that nothing was wasted. Their camp cookery would have to be even more simple than ours, for they had not yet discovered the use of metals, so could not have a three-legged cauldron. They boiled their water in a very curious manner, by dropping red-hot stones into it. It must have taken a long time and given rather a funny flavour to the joints, but no doubt they tasted delicious to Neolithic appetites."

"I'd like to restore a few of the huts, and come and live in them for a few days, and pretend we were primitive folk," said Deirdre.

"Mrs. Trevellyan has often talked of excavating them," remarked Miss Birks. "I hope she will do so. It is quite possible that some very interesting relics of the Stone Age might be turned up. It would probably fix the period when they were inhabited."

"How long ago would that be?" asked one of the girls.

"Most likely about two thousand years or more."

The conversation at this point was interrupted, for in the distance appeared Miss Herbert, running, beckoning and calling to them all at once. In considerable alarm they went to meet her.

"Where's Ronnie?" she gasped. "I've lost him! Oh, has anybody seen him? Is he here with you?"

"He's certainly not here," said Miss Birks. "We've not seen him since we met you an hour or more ago. When did you miss him, and where?"

"On the beach," sobbed Miss Herbert hysterically. "He was playing with his little shrimping net. I sat down to read my book, and I kept looking to see that he was all right, and then suddenly he had disappeared. I thought he must have trotted back round the point, so I followed, but I couldn't find him. I hoped he'd come up here to you. It's very naughty of him to run away."

"We must find him at once," said Miss Birks gravely. "Girls, you had better go in parties of three, each in a different direction. Miss Barlow and I will go with Miss Herbert. We won't give up the search until he is found."

"Did he go round the other corner of the cove?" asked Gerda.

"He couldn't. The waves were dashing quite high against the rocks. I'm sure he would never venture," declared the distracted governess.

"He's such a plucky little chap, he would venture anything."

"Oh, surely not! He couldn't! He couldn't have gone there! He may have run home!"

"Better not waste any more time, but go and see what's become of him," suggested Miss Birks rather dryly. She had always thought Miss Herbert too easy-going where Ronnie was concerned.

The bands of searchers set off in eight different directions, shouting, hallooing, cuckooing, and making every kind of call likely to attract the child's attention. Some took the beach and some the cliffs, while others ran to the Castle to see if he had returned to the garden. There had never been such a hue and cry on the headland. That Ronnie should be lost was an unparalleled disaster, and considering the many accidents which might possibly have happened to him, each of his friends searched with a deadly fear in her heart. Gerda, her once rosy face white as chalk, had flown along the cliffs with Deirdre and Dulcie, shouting his name again and again.

"He may have gone round the west corner, though Miss Herbert says he couldn't," she panted. "Let us get on to the cliff above, where we can look down. Oh, Ronnie! Ronnie! Cuckoo! Where are you? Cooee!"

As Gerda gave the last long-drawn-out call she stopped suddenly and motioned the others to silence. From the shore below there came a faint but quite unmistakable response. Creeping to the verge of the overhanging precipice Gerda peeped down. There, at a distance of forty feet beneath, stood Ronnie, a pathetic little figure, turning up a small frightened face and quavering a shrill "Cooee!" His position was one of imminent danger. The point round which he had scrambled half an hour before was now covered with great dashing waves that hurled their spray high into the air, and the narrow strip of shingle upon which he stood was rapidly growing smaller and smaller as the tide advanced. On either hand escape was impossible; behind him roared the sea, and in front towered the steep unscalable face of the cliff.

"Gerda! Gerda!" he wailed piteously.

Gerda turned to her companions almost like an animal at bay. Her lips were white as her cheeks, her eyes blazed. "We must save him!" she choked.

"The life-boat! Let us fetch the life-boat!" cried Deirdre. "You stay here and I'll run to Pontperran. Some of the others will go with me; Annie Pridwell is a fast runner. Cooee! Cooee! Ronnie is found!"

Deirdre was very swift of foot and darted off like a hare, shouting her message to the nearest band of searchers. In an incredibly short space of time the news had spread, and all were hurrying towards the cliff. The ill tidings reached Mrs. Trevellyan at the Castle, and, sick with anxiety, she hastened to the spot, first sending one of her men to urge speed in launching the life-boat. The tide was sweeping in fast, and nearer and nearer crept the cruel, hungry waves, as if thirsting to snatch the little figure huddled at the foot of the cliff. Ronnie was too worn out and too frightened to call now; he lay watching the advancing water with terror-stricken blue eyes, still grasping the shrimping net that had led him to this disaster.

Could the life-boat possibly arrive in time? That was the question which each spectator asked dumbly, not daring to voice it in words. Nearer and ever nearer swept the waves. Where there had been yards of shingle there were only feet; soon it was a matter of inches. There was not a sign of any boat to be seen. A sea-crow below flapped its wings like an omen of death.

"Tom and Smith have gone to fetch ropes," breathed Miss Birks, and her voice broke the strain of almost intolerable silence.

"There's not time to wait for them."

"Can we do nothing?"

"Oh, is there no way to save him?"

Then Gerda stood up, with a sudden light shining in her clear eyes.

"Yes, yes!" she cried. "There's the old windlass! I'm going down to him by that!"

Years ago there had been a small find of china clay on the headland. It had been lowered in buckets over the side of the cliff to be taken away by boat, and the remains of the apparatus, a derelict, rickety affair, stood within a few yards of the place where the watchers were gathered. A rusty bucket was still attached to the frayed, weather-worn rope twisted round the roller. To descend by so frail a support was indeed a risk so great that only the most desperate necessity could justify it. A general murmur of horror arose from those assembled.

"It's the one chance—I'm going to try it," repeated Gerda. "You can lower me gently by the handle. I'm going to save him—or die with him."

She began rapidly to unwind the windlass so as to allow the bucket to reach the edge of the cliff. Realizing that she was in grim earnest, the others offered no further objection, and came eagerly to her assistance. She had seized the rope and was about to step into the bucket when a strong hand put her aside. The stranger in the brown jersey had silently joined himself to the group.

"This is my place," he said firmly. "I am going down the cliff. Hold hard, there! Pay out the rope gently and don't let me go with a run or I'm done for. Easy! Easy! Give me more rope when I call."

So quickly did he substitute himself for Gerda that he was over the edge of the cliff almost before anyone had realized what was taking place. The onlookers held their breath as they watched the perilous descent. The bucket swayed from side to side and bumped against the rock, but holding on to the rope with one hand the man managed with the other to keep himself from injury. Down—down—down he swung, till, clear of the cliff, he dangled, as it seemed, in mid-air.

"Now, rope! More rope!" he called. "Quicker!"

The windlass creaked on the rusty axle, there was a rush, a drop, then a shout of triumph. The next moment he had snatched Ronnie in his arms. Ringing cheers reached him from above, but the battle was only half won after all. There was still no sign of the life-boat; a wave swept already over his feet. The only road to safety lay up the cliffside. Would the old weather-worn rope stand the double strain? There was no time for questioning. Telling Ronnie to hold on tightly round his neck he once more entered the bucket and gave the signal for the ascent. To the anxious hearts of the watchers the next few minutes seemed an eternity. Those at the windlass turned the handle slowly and steadily in response to the shouts from below. If there had been danger before, the peril now was trebled. With a child clinging round his neck it was far more difficult for the stranger to keep clear of the rock. The old worn-out machine creaked and groaned like one in mortal agony. Life or death hung on the strength of a rusted piece of chain and a half-rotten hempen rope. Up! Up! Up! Would the suspense never end? Only a few yards now and the watchers were waiting to help. Once more the rickety axle creaked and shivered, then the stranger's head and shoulders appeared over the edge of the cliff, and eager hands grasped him and pulled him gently forward on to firm ground. He had lost his hat in the descent, and now the sunlight fell full on his clear-cut features and his fair, closely-cropped hair.

"You—L'Estrange! You! You!" shrieked Mrs. Trevellyan wildly.

But for answer he placed Ronnie in her arms, and pushing his way through the excited group ran off over the warren and was out of sight before the lookers-on had recovered from their amazement. By the time the life-boat had made its way round the coast from Pontperran harbour great breakers were crashing against the face of the rock with a dull booming and showers of foam, as if angry to have been cheated of their prey.

"No one could live for a moment in this cruel sea!" exclaimed Deirdre, shuddering with horror as she thought how the fierce water would have dashed and tossed and crushed the little helpless figure left to the mercy of the waves.

"Ronnie will be doubly dear to us now," said Miss Birks, marshalling her girls together and turning to leave the cliff.

CHAPTER XVI

Hare and Hounds

AFTER the intense excitement of Ronnie's peril and subsequent rescue, his friends at the Dower House found it a little difficult to settle down into ordinary school routine. They could discuss no other topic, and many were their speculations concerning the brown-jerseyed stranger who had appeared in the very nick of time, and vanished afterwards without waiting to be thanked. His identity had not been disclosed, and when the girls spoke of him, Miss Birks, rather to their surprise, dismissed the subject hurriedly.

"If he does not wish his brave deed to be acknowledged, we must respect his silence," she said. "It is useless and futile to go further into the matter."

Mrs. Trevellyan was for a few days prostrated from the effects of that half-hour of suspense, but she had sufficiently recovered to attend church on Sunday, and holding Ronnie's little hand tightly in hers, knelt in the old Castle pew, with bent head and tears raining down her cheeks, as the clergyman announced that a member of the congregation desired to return special thanks for a very great mercy vouchsafed to her during the past week. Others besides Mrs. Trevellyan joined with heart-felt gratitude in that addition to the general thanksgiving, and when afterwards the lines of the grand old hymn rang out—

"O God, our help in ages past,Our hope for years to come",

there was not a girl in the Dower House pews who did not sing it with real meaning in the words.

On the Monday, Mrs. Trevellyan, hoping to recover from her nervous attack more easily if she were out of sight of the sea, went away for a short visit to an inland watering-place, taking Ronnie and poor contrite Miss Herbert, who could not forgive herself for having allowed her young charge to run into danger. Appreciating the wisdom of the step, and realizing that her own girls had been in a state of high tension, and were suffering from the consequent reaction, Miss Birks granted the school a whole holiday, and took votes on how the day should be spent. Opinions seemed divided, so it was finally decided that Forms VI and VAshould go by train to Linsgarth, look over the ruins of the abbey, and walk home by road; while VB, containing the younger and more wildly energetic spirits, should enjoy the pleasures of a game at hare and hounds.

It was years since a paper chase had been held at the school, and while the elder girls affected to despise it, the younger ones had plumped for it in a body. They felt they required something more stirring than admiring ruins and marching along a high road.

"It may be very cultured, and good taste, and intellectual, and all the rest of it, to poke round with Miss Birks among Norman arches and broken choir-stalls, but it doesn't work off steam," confessed Evie Bennett. "I'm longing for a good sporting run, and that's the fact!"

"Let the Sixth talk architectural jargon if they like; hard exercise for me!" agreed Betty Scott.

It was arranged that all should start out at ten o'clock; Miss Birks conducting the expedition to Linsgarth, and Miss Harding assuming command of the paper chase, while Mademoiselle, who was a bad walker and disliked country excursions, promised herself a delightful day of rest and leisure in the garden. Miss Birks insisted that there must be three "hares", all solemnly pledged to keep well together, and the remaining six, who were to be "hounds", had orders not to outstrip Miss Harding to the extent of getting hopelessly out of eyeshot and earshot. Fortunately Miss Harding was energetic and enthusiastic, and promised not to be a drag on the proceedings. She donned her shortest skirt and her coolest jumper, and discarding a hat, appeared fully ready to play as hearty a part in the game as any of her pupils.

Everybody, naturally, was anxious to act "hare", so it was decided that the fairest plan was to draw lots for the coveted posts. The three fortunate papers with the crosses fell to Deirdre, Gerda, and Annie Pridwell.

"I'm not jealous, but I do envy you dreadfully," confessed Evie Bennett. "Oh, I'm not grumbling! I'm ready to take my sporting luck, and someone must draw the blanks. You'll make capital hares, because you're all good runners and don't lose your breath quickly. But, I beseech you, don't go too fast! Remember, the hounds are tied to Miss Harding's apron-string. It's no fun if we can't catch a glimpse of you the whole run. And, please, do a little backwards-and-forwards work, cross a brook, or double round a wood—anything to make it more difficult to find the scent. We don't want to be home in a couple of hours."

"Trust us to be as cunning as foxes," declared Annie Pridwell. "I'm an old hand at the game. We play it in the holidays at home."

"I haven't Annie's experience, but I can run," said Deirdre.

"So you can, best of anyone in the school, and Gerda's no slacker, so I think you'll do."

Each girl had a packet of sandwiches and a small folding drinking-cup, so that they could take some refreshment when they felt hungry. Miss Birks had arranged that a cold lunch should be laid in the dining-hall at the Dower House at one o'clock, and left on the table indefinitely, so as to be ready for the girls when they came in, whether early or late, and those who returned first were to help themselves without waiting for the others.

"We shall all feel far more at liberty with this plan," she said. "It spoils everyone's pleasure to have to hurry home by a certain time. It is much more enjoyable to think we have the day free to do as we like. We can have tea together in the evening, and compare our experiences."

"We shall have seen something worth seeing," declared the senior girls.

"Ah, but you won't have had the ripping, glorious time that we mean to have!" retorted the members of VB.

Punctually at ten o'clock the three hares were ready, each with a satchel round her shoulder containing the scraps of torn paper that were to provide the scent. They were to have ten minutes' start, after which the hounds would follow in full cry. They had decided among themselves what route to take, and, determined to give the hunt a run, they selected the direction of Kergoff, and set off towards the old windmill, where in the early spring they had surveyed the country to draw maps, as a lesson in practical geography. There was a definite reason for their choice, as the windmill could be approached by no less than three separate paths, and by dodging from one to another of these they hoped very successfully to puzzle their pursuers.

"We'll leave some scent by the gate of Perkins's farm," said the experienced Annie; "then, of course, they'll think we've chosen the road past the quarry. But we'll only go a little way up the lane, then climb the wall, cross the fields, and get into the upper road, leave a scent there, then track through the wood, and go past the old yew tree by the path over the tor."

"There'll be a scent on each separate path," chuckled Deirdre. "They'll be a good long time in finding out which to follow. We must be careful not to let ourselves be seen when we're crossing the tor."

There was a delightful interest in baffling the hounds; it seemed to hold almost the thrill of earlier and more romantic times.

"Can you imagine the moss-troopers are after you?" asked Deirdre; "or that you've slain the Red King, or robbed an abbot in the greenwood, and are fleeing for your life to take sanctuary in the nearest church?"

"No, I'm a smuggler," said Annie, "trying to outwit the coast-guardsmen, and arrange to leave my kegs of brandy and packets of tea and yards of French lace in some cunning hiding-place. What are you, Gerda?"

"An escaped prisoner from Dartmoor, running from his warders?" queried Deirdre. "That would be sport!"

"There's a warrant out for your arrest, and you're dodging the officers of the law," laughed Annie lightly.

But Gerda did not appear to accept the suggestions kindly, or in the spirit of fun in which they were intended. To the girls' surprise she blushed, just as she used to do when first she came to school, and looked so clearly annoyed instead of amused that the joke fell flat. She was never at any time talkative, but now, taking seeming offence at these very innocent remarks, she drew into her innermost shell, and refused to converse at all. Knowing her of old in this uncommunicative mood, the others did not trouble further, but left her to her own devices until she chose to come out of it. They had found by experience that it was useless either to question her, laugh at her, or rally her upon her silence; the more they pressed the subject the more obstinate she would grow. It was no great hardship to miss her out of their talk; they much preferred each other's company without an unwelcome third.

"Those that sulk for nothing may sulk, so far as I'm concerned," remarked Deirdre pointedly.

"I hate people not to be able to take the least scrap of a joke," said Annie. "Why, Betty and Evie and I are teasing each other the whole time in our bedroom."

"You three certainly know how to rag."

"Rather! We'd die of dullness if we didn't."

All the time they went the "hares" were carefully carrying out their policy of puzzling those who followed. Backwards and forwards, across small brooks, through woods and thickets, over field, farm-yard, and common they laid the most bewildering of scents, more than enough to satisfy the demands of Evie Bennett, and sufficient indeed to make her declare it almost an impossibility to decide on the right track. All this artful dodging, however, had necessitated scattering a large number of the precious handfuls of paper, and by the time they arrived at the old windmill they found to their consternation that the contents of the three satchels were almost exhausted.

"What are we to do?" asked Annie tragically. "We can't go on and leave no scents! Are we to sit here on the windmill steps, and let ourselves be run to earth when we've only done half the round?"

It was a crisis indeed, and Deirdre could not see any way out of the difficulty. She stood ruefully contemplating her empty bag, and looking utterly baffled. It was Gerda, after all, who came to the rescue with a valuable suggestion.

"We're close to that queer old house," she said. "Don't you remember how we climbed in through the window, and found all those letters lying about upstairs? They can't be wanted, or somebody would have taken them away. Let's go and see if they're still there, and commandeer what we like."

"Gerda, you're a genius!" shrieked Annie. "We'll go this second. Why, it's the very thing we want!"

It was no great distance to the old house. Down the corkscrew road they ran, through the small fir wood, and over the river by the stone bridge. "Forster's Folly" looked if possible even more tumbledown and dilapidated than when they had visited it in February. The spring gales had blown down many more slates and made a gap in the roof; the creepers in their summer luxuriance almost hid the broken windows; large patches of stucco had fallen from the walls; a chimney-pot lay smashed on the front walk; one of the props of the long veranda had been swept away by the whirling stream, leaving the flooring in a dangerous condition; and the crop of nettles and brambles in the garden had outgrown all bounds and, smothering the original privet hedge, overflowed into the road.

"It's more spooky and Rat's Hall-y and Moated Grange-y than ever!" declared Annie. "I could imagine there'd been a witches' carnival since we were last here, or a dance of ghouls. Ugh! I'm all in a shiver at having to go inside! Suppose we find the ghost after all?"

"I'll chance ghosts," said Deirdre. "I'd be a great deal more frightened to find a tramp there!"

"Oh, surely even a tramp wouldn't spend a night in such a haunted den! Still, it's so deserted, it might be a place for smugglers or coiners or burglars. Oh, I don't think I dare go in after all! No, I daren't!"

Annie was half-serious, and looking inclined to turn tail.

"Don't show the white feather now," said Gerda reproachfully. "Where are we to get our paper from?"

"Come along, Annie, and don't be an idiot!" was Deirdre's uncomplimentary rejoinder. "Why, you were the first to go in before!"

"My nerves were stronger last February," protested Annie. "I'll let one of you take the lead this time."

It was quite a pilgrimage through the nettle-grown garden to reach the window where they had made their entrance into the house. It was open, just as they had left it, but long trails of clematis swept across, and there was an empty bird's nest on the corner of the sill. It did not appear as if anyone had disturbed its quiet for months. This time Gerda led the way, with a confidence and assurance that rather surprised the other two. Through the dilapidated dining-room, along the dim mouldy hall and up the creaking stairs they tramped, trying by the noise they made to dispel the ghostly feeling that clung to the deserted old place. If coiners, smugglers, or burglars had visited the house, they had left no trace of their presence. Everything on the story above was untouched, though perhaps a trifle more dust-covered and cobwebby than before. Gerda darted upon the bathful of old letters, and with eager fingers anxiously began turning them hurriedly over.

"Haven't time to sort them out," declared Annie, snatching up a handful and putting them into her bag. "I vote we take what we want, and tear them up outside. Why are you looking at them so particularly, Gerda?"

"I thought some might have crests. Do let me see what you've taken!" said Gerda beseechingly. "No, I don't want these!"

"Why, you've never looked inside the envelopes! How can you tell whether they've crests?"

"Oh, never mind! It doesn't matter!" Gerda was on the floor, searching among some opened and torn sheets that lay on the mouldering straw.

"Look here! We can't stay all day while you read old Forster's correspondence! We've got enough! Come along!"

"One minute! Oh, do wait for me a second! I'll come! Yes, I'll come in half a jiffy!"

"We'll go without you, then you'll soon trot after us," said Deirdre, who had filled her satchel. She and Annie clattered downstairs again, looked into the empty kitchen, and dared each other to peep into the dark hall cupboard. They had hardly waited more than a minute in the dining-room when Gerda joined them.

"Well, have you found the orthodox long-lost will?" mocked Annie.

"I've got enough scent to take us back to Pontperran, and that's what I wanted," retorted Gerda, with a light in her eyes that seemed almost more than the occasion justified.

No more time must be lost if they did not want to be run to earth by the hounds, so returning to the windmill steps they tore up their fresh supply of paper, taking bites of their sandwiches while they did so. A loud "Cuckoo!" in the distance caused all three to start to their feet in alarm, and leaving a trail behind the broken sail, they scrambled over a fence, and dived down through a coppice which led to the stream. They followed the bank for some distance before they judged it safe once more to take to a foot-path, then doubling round the hill on which the windmill stood, they tacked off in the direction of Kergoff.

The hounds reached the Dower House at five o'clock, exactly half an hour after the hares, and over a combined luncheon-tea discussed the run, and universally agreed that the day had been "ripping".

The Sixth and VA, rather puffed up with their archæological researches, tried to be superior and instructive, and to give their juniors a digest of what they had learnt at the abbey. But at this VB rebelled.

"You've had your fun, and we've had ours," said Annie. "Don't try and cram architecture down our throats. I tell you frankly, I can't tell the difference between a Norman arch and any other kind of one, and I don't want to!"

"You utter ignoramus!"

"I'm a good hare, if I'm nothing else!" chuckled Annie. "We must have led them a run of about fourteen miles!"

"Deirdre, I want to ask you something," said Gerda that evening. "You remember that crest you took before from Forster's Folly? Will you swop it with me for some chocolates?"

"Why, I'll give it to you if you like," returned Deirdre, who was in an amiable, after-tea frame of mind, and disposed towards generosity. "I'm tired of crest collecting, and I've taken up stamps. Here it is! It's been in my jewel-box since the day I got it. Are you going in for crests?"

"They're my latest and absolutely dearest hobby," declared Gerda emphatically.

CHAPTER XVII

A Discovery

AFTER the delightful dissipation of a whole day's holiday, Miss Birks demanded a period of solid work from her pupils, and deeming that she had sufficiently satisfied their craving for excitement, took no notice of either hints or headaches, but enforced preparation and practising with, as Dulcie expressed it, "a total lack of all consideration". Dulcie, never a remarkably hard worker at any season, was more than usually prone to "slack" in summer, and it needed the combined energies of Miss Birks, Miss Harding, and Mademoiselle to keep her up to the mark. It was more than ever necessary to maintain the standard at present, for examination week was drawing near, and this year several extra prizes were offered for competition. Mrs. Trevellyan had promised a beautiful edition of Tennyson's poems for the best paper on English literature, the Vicar added a handsome volume of *Pictures from Palestine* for the most correct answers to Scripture History, and Mademoiselle herself proffered a copy of *Lettres de mon Moulin* for the most spirited declamation of any piece of French poetry not less than two hundred lines in length, the quality of the accent to be particularly taken into account. These were in addition to the usual annual rewards for mathematics, languages, English history, music, drawing, and needlecraft, so that among so many various subjects each girl might feel that she had at least some chance of winning success. At the eleventh hour the Principal announced that a prize would be given for general improvement.

"That's to make slackers like you buck up, Dulcie!" declared Annie Pridwell.

"Really, I wish Miss Birks would offer a prize for pure English," said Jessie Macpherson, who happened to overhear. "The slang you V_B talk is outrageous. Your whole conversation seems made up of 'ripping' and 'scrumptious' and 'spiffing' and other silly words that don't mean anything. I tell you, slang's going out of fashion, even at public schools, and you're behind the times."

"Don't be a prig, Jessie. What else can I call Dulcie except a slacker? Am I to say she shows a languorous disinclination for close application, and advise her to exert her mental activities? It would sound like a 'Catechism' from a Young Ladies' Seminary of a hundred years ago!"

"There is one comfort in having worked badly," admitted Dulcie. "If I make a spurt now, I shall show more 'marked improvement' than if I'd been jogging along steadily all the time."

"Ah, but the tortoise won the race while the hare slept!" retorted Jessie.

In view of the forthcoming music examination, practising was performed with double diligence, and from 6 a.m. to 8.30 p.m. the strains of Schumann's "Arabesque", Tschaikowsky's "Chanson Triste", or Rachmaninoff's "Prelude", the three test pieces, echoed pretty constantly through the house, in varying degrees of proficiency.

"It's a good thing nobody belonging to the school has to do the judging," said Emily Northwood, as she stood in the hall listening to the conflicting sounds of three pianos. "Even Miss Birks must be so sick of these particular pieces that she could hardly express a fair opinion on them. Dr. Harvey James will come fresh to the fray."

The organist and choirmaster of the collegiate church at Wexminster, being a doctor of music, was regarded as a very suitable examiner for the occasion, and even if his standard proved high, all at least would have the same chance, for he had not visited the school before, and therefore could regard nobody with special favour. He was a new resident in the district, and Miss Birks hoped next term to arrange for him to come over weekly and give lessons to her more advanced pupils, who would be likely to appreciate his musical knowledge and profit by his teaching.

The thought of having to play before their prospective music master spurred on most of the girls even more than the chance of the prize; they dashed valiantly at difficult passages, counted diligently, and loosened their muscles with five-finger exercises, each anxious to be placed in the rank of those sufficiently advanced to be transferred to his tuition. The drawing students also, though they could not practise specially for their own prize, were busy finishing copies and sketches for a small exhibition of work done during the school year, which was to be held in one of the classrooms during examination week, and criticized by Mr. Leonard Pearce, an artist who had consented to set and judge the competition. Miss Harding was urging increased attention to mathematics, Miss Birks was giving extra coaching in history and English literature, Mademoiselle was hacking away at languages till her pupils almost wished that French and German were as dead as ancient Egyptian and Assyrian, so it was a very busy little world at the Dower House, so busy that really nobody had time to think of anything else. The Principal, anxious to keep her flock in good health, insisted upon the recreation hours being devoted to definite exercise, and either games or organized walks under the supervision of a mistress were compulsory.

For the present there was no strolling about the warren in "threesomes", there were no visits to the headland, or rambles on the beach. The girls grumbled a little at this lack of their accustomed freedom, complained that set walks reminded them of a penitentiary, and declared that to be obliged to play cricket took all the fun out of it. They thrived on the system, however, and were able to manage the increased brain work demanded from them without incurring the penalty of headaches, backaches, or loss of appetite. A few certainly pleaded minor ailments as an excuse for shirking, but Miss Birks's long experience had taught her to distinguish readily between real illness and shamming, and she dismissed the would-be invalids each with a dose of such a nauseous compound as entirely to discourage them from seeking further sympathy. Her bottle, a harmless mixture of Turkey rhubarb and carbonate of magnesia, might have been a magic elixir for the relief of all diseases, for with the same marvellous rapidity it cured Francie's palpitations, Irene's dyspepsia, and Elyned's attacks of faintness.

"Nasty, filthy stuff!" declared the indignant sufferers, who, with a remembrance of Miss Birks's treatment of the measles patients, had fondly expected to be coddled and cosseted, regaled on soda-water and lemonade, and forbidden to overexert themselves.

"Serve you right!" chuckled their friends. "It's your own faults, for you couldn't expect Miss Birks to believe in your whines when you look in such absolutely rude health, and compass your meals so creditably. Why didn't you refuse all solid food?"

"Oh no, thank you!"

"And declare cocoa made you shudder?"

"That's beyond a joke."

"If anybody looks ill in this house," continued Annie, "it's Mademoiselle. She's pale and thin, if you like, and eats next to nothing, but she doesn't make any fuss about it."

Noticeably Mademoiselle's increased work and anxiety on behalf of her pupils' success had a bad effect on her health. She looked worn and overdone, and there were dark circles round her tired eyes. Though she did not complain, she confessed to being troubled with sleeplessness. Night after night she lay awake till daybreak, and was sometimes only dropping into a doze when the getting-up bell clanged in the passage. "*Nuits blanches* may be all very well in music, but they are not pleasant when one experiences them," she confided to Miss Harding. "When I stay waiting for sleep, I hear many curious sounds. Yes—such as one does not hear during the daylight."

"A house is always full of creaks and groans if one stays awake at night," returned Miss Harding. "You mustn't mind them."

"During the day I smile at them," continued Mademoiselle, "but if I keep vigil I am nervous. Yes, to-night I shall be very nervous, for Miss Birks will be away. I like not that she be away."

It was very seldom that the Principal gave herself a holiday during the term, but for once she was going to London to attend an important educational meeting, and would spend the night in town. She started by an early train, leaving her small kingdom in perfect order, and confident that for so short a space of time nothing could possibly go wrong. Certainly nothing ought to have gone wrong; her arrangements were excellent, and Miss Harding was thoroughly capable of acting deputy during her absence. Yet there is an old proverb that "while the cat's away the mice will play", and the mere fact that she was not on the spot made a difference in the school. The girls did not give any trouble, but there was a feeling of relaxed discipline in the air.

At four o'clock, instead of going straight from their classroom to their practising, Deirdre and Dulcie decided to indulge in the luxury of a run round the grounds first. They walked briskly through the shrubbery, down the steps, and along the terrace, till they came to the kitchen-garden. Now this kitchen-garden was absolutely forbidden territory to the girls, and they had never been inside it. To-day the gate, which was generally locked, stood temptingly open. It seemed an opportunity too good to be resisted. With one accord they threw rules to the winds, and decided to explore.

A thick and high holly hedge effectually screened this corner of the grounds from wind, and guarded it from intruders. It was a warm, productive plot of land, and entirely provided the school with fruit and vegetables. Deirdre and Dulcie did not trouble about the currants and gooseberries, but kept straight down the path. They wished particularly to investigate the far end. Here the garden abutted on the cliffs, which sloped downward in a series of zigzag ridges.

The girls made their way gingerly over a freshly-prepared bed of young cabbages to the borderland where rhubarb and horse-radish merged into wormwood and ragwort. It was perfectly easy to slip over the edge and begin to go down the first long shelving slab of rock. There was a drop of about four feet on to the second shelf, which again sloped downwards at a gentle level to a third. Here the cliff ended in a precipice, so steep that even the most experienced climber could not descend without a rope. Rather baffled, the two girls crept cautiously along the edge, then Deirdre suddenly gave a whoop of delight, for she had spied a rough flight of steps cut in the surface of the rock, and evidently leading to the beach below. It was rather a cat's staircase to venture upon, but they were possessed with a thirst for exploration, and were not easily to be daunted. Deirdre went first, and shouted encouragement to her chum, and Dulcie picked up heart to follow, so that in the course of a few minutes they found themselves safely on the sands at the bottom.

"Whew! It's like climbing down the ladder of a lighthouse," exclaimed Dulcie, subsiding on to a convenient stone. Her legs were shaking in a most unaccountable fashion, and her breath coming and going far more rapidly than was comfortable.

"It might have been worse," affirmed Deirdre, trying not to show that her nerve had in any degree failed her, and surveying the scene with the eye of a prospector.

They were in a small and very narrow cove, so hidden between cliffs which jutted out overhead that it was practically invisible from above, and certainly could not be seen from anywhere in the school grounds. It was a pretty little creek, with a silvery slip of beach, and green clumps of ferns growing high up in the interstices of the rocks; quite a romantic spot, so beautiful and secluded that it might almost be the haunt of a mermaiden or a water nixie. The ferns, which were flourishing in unusual luxuriance, caught Deirdre's attention.

"I believe it's the sea-spleenwort," she remarked. "Don't you remember we found some at Kergoff, and Miss Birks was so excited about it? I'm sure she doesn't know all this is growing at the very bottom of her own garden. I'll try and get a root."

To obtain a root was more easily said than done, however. Most of the clumps of fern were in very inaccessible situations, and too deeply embedded in the rock to be removed. Deirdre climbed from one to

THE SCHOOL BY THE SEA

another in vain, then noticing a particularly fine group of fronds on a projecting shelf far above her head, commenced to scale the cliff. She reached the shelf fairly easily, but instead of setting to work to try to uproot the fern, she gave a long whistle of surprise.

"What's the matter?" asked Dulcie from below.

"Matter! Come up yourself and see! Oh, goody!"

Dulcie was still a little shaky, but spurred on by curiosity she got up the cliff somehow, and added a "Hallo!" of amazement to her chum's exclamations. Facing them was the entrance to a cave. At one time it had evidently been carefully blocked up, but now the wooden boarding that guarded it had been wrenched asunder, leaving a small opening just sufficient to enter by. The girls peeped cautiously in, but beyond the first few yards all was dark. This was indeed a discovery. The mouth of the cave was so effectually hidden by the crags which surrounded it that nobody would have suspected its existence who had not come across it by accident. What secrets lay in its mysterious depths, who could say? Thrilled with excitement, the girls turned to one another.

"If we could only explore it!" breathed Dulcie.

"We're going to!" returned Deirdre firmly. "I shall run back this instant to the house for a candle. You wait here."

Deirdre's impatience made short work of the cat's staircase. She scrambled up the rocks like a squirrel, and was soon racing up the kitchen-garden. To secure her bedroom candle and a box of matches was the work of a few minutes. As she pelted impetuously downstairs again, she nearly fell over Gerda, who had been doing preparation in the schoolroom, and scattered the pile of books she was carrying.

"Do be careful," said the latter in remonstrance. "Where are you going in such a hurry? And what do you want with your candle?"

"Never you mind! It's no business of yours!" retorted Deirdre, running away without even an apology.

Gerda picked up her books and carried them upstairs, but instead of continuing her preparation she went to the window. She was just in time to catch a glimpse of Deirdre vanishing down the kitchen-garden. The sight seemed to afford her food for thought. She stood for a moment or two lost in indecision, then, evidently making up her mind, she set off in pursuit of her school-fellow. Deirdre, meanwhile, returned to the cove with speed and agility, and found Dulcie waiting where she had left her.

"I had a horrible feeling that a monster might come out while you were away!" she declared. "Do you think we dare go in?"

"Dare? Of course we dare! I'm not going to have fetched this candle for nothing. Dulcie Wilcox, where's your pluck? Come along this minute, or I'll not be chums with you again. Here, you may hold the matches."

Having lighted the candle, the two girls stepped through the breach in the wooden barricade, and commenced their exploration. The passage, high at first, soon lowered till it was little above their heads, and narrowed to a width of barely three feet. The walls, which for the first ten yards were worn as if by the action of the sea, became more jagged, and had plainly been hewn out with the aid of a pick, the natural cavern having been greatly extended. Here and there the floor was wet, and the roof showed an oozy deposit as if some surface spring were forcing itself through the strata of the rock. On and on the girls went for two hundred yards or more, Deirdre going first and holding the candle well in front of her, so as to see the way. It was delightfully exciting, yet there was a thrill of horror about it, for who could tell what might be lurking round the next corner? Dulcie's nerves were strung to such a pitch that she was ready to scream at the least alarm. Not a sound, however, broke the dead silence. The passage in its lonely calm might have been the entrance to an Egyptian tomb.

"Does it lead anywhere?" whispered Dulcie. "Oh! hadn't we better turn back? We've gone far enough."

"I'm going to the end, if it's in Australia!" replied Deirdre, and having possession of the candle, she was in a position to dictate.

A few extra yards, however, concluded their journey, the passage being once again blocked by a wooden barrier. This was more carefully constructed than the one at the entrance, being made of well-planed timber, and fitted with a door, which stood half-way open, and led into a rough kind of chamber, rather resembling the crypt of a church. At the far side of this there was a small closed door.

"Well, we've got into a queer place!" exclaimed Deirdre. "Must have been a smuggler's cellar, I should say. No doubt they used to keep kegs and kegs of brandy down here in the good old days. Look, the roof is vaulted over there! Where does that door lead to?"

The little door in question had apparently been opened by force, to judge from the broken lock and the marks of some sharp instrument on the jambs. At present it was closed, but not fastened. What lay beyond? With a feeling that they had arrived at the crowning-point of their adventure, Deirdre opened it and peeped in. She found herself looking down from an eminence of about four feet into a bedroom. The room was in complete darkness, for the window was barred with heavy wooden shutters, but by the aid of her candle she could see it was unoccupied. Giving the light to Dulcie to hold, she cautiously descended, then aided her chum to follow. The door through which they had stepped formed part of the panelling over the mantelpiece, and when closed with its original spring would no doubt have been indistinguishable from the rest of the woodwork. The room, though neglected and in great disorder, nevertheless bore traces of recent habitation. The bed, with its tumbled blankets, had certainly been slept in. On the dressing-table, spread out on a newspaper, were the remains of a meal. A small oil cooking-stove held a kettle, and one or two little packets, probably containing tea and sugar, lay about. On the floor, torn into small pieces, were the shreds of a letter written in German. Dusty and untended as it was now, the room must once have been pretty, and bore strong evidence of the ownership of a little girl. On the walls hung framed colour prints of Millais's "Cherry Ripe", "Little Mrs. Gamp", "Little Red Riding Hood", and "Miss Muffet". In the corner stood a doll's house, a doll's cradle, and a miniature chest of drawers. A chiffonier seemed to be a repository for numerous treasures—a set of tiny alabaster cups and saucers, a glass globe which when shaken reproduced a snowstorm inside, a writing-desk, a walnut work-box, a small Japanese cabinet, and a whole row of juvenile books. Deirdre took up some of the latter, blew the dust off and examined them. They were volumes of *Little Folks* and *Chatterbox* of many years ago. On the title-page of each was written: "To darling Lillie from Father and Mother".

In greatest amazement the girls wandered round the room, looking first at one thing, then at another. How old the dust was that mostly covered them! Here and there it had been hastily swept away, to make a clearance for cup and saucer or provisions, but in general the little possessions were untouched. Even some New Year cards stood on the chest of drawers, bearing greetings and good wishes for the coming season.

"I want to see better," said Deirdre. "This wretched candle only gives half a light. I've never been in such a fascinating place. Help me, Dulcie, and we'll try and unfasten the shutters."

The heavy iron bar was old and rusty. It must have been in its place for many a long year. For some time the girls pushed and tugged in vain, then with a mighty effort they dislodged it from its socket, and let it clatter down. Deirdre slowly swung aside the shutter. After the faint light of their one candle, the flood of sunshine which burst in completely dazzled them. As soon as they could see, they peeped out through the dingy panes of glass. To their immense surprise they found they were looking into the Dower House garden. Then Deirdre suddenly realized the truth.

"Dulcie! Dulcie!" she cried, "I verily believe we're in the barred room!"

There seemed little doubt about the matter, when they came to consider it. The position of the window corresponded exactly with the closed-up one which had always faced them from the tennis-courts, and whose secret they had so often discussed. The mystery, instead of becoming clearer, seemed only to deepen. Why was one of the bedrooms in the Dower House filled with a child's possessions and sealed with iron bars, yet accessible from a cave on the beach, and evidently in present occupation?

The daylight revealed its extraordinary condition with great clearness; the dust, dirt, and cobwebs looked forlorn in the extreme. On a hook on the door, which presumably led into the Dower House landing, hung a net filled with hard wooden balls, and as the draught blew in from the opening over the fireplace, these swayed about and knocked with a gentle rapping against the panel.

"There's your ghost, Dulcie," said Deirdre. "That was the tap-tapping you heard in the passage. It wasn't a spook after all, you see."

"You were just as scared as I was," protested Dulcie. "I think I'm rather scared now. Let's go! Suppose whoever's been here making tea were to come back? I believe I'd have hysterics."

There was something in Dulcie's suggestion. It had not before occurred to Deirdre that it would be unpleasant if the owner of the kettle were to return and demand an explanation of their presence.

"We must put the shutters back," she decreed.

This was easier said than done, but after considerable trouble they managed to restore the room once more to its former state of darkness. Their candle was burning rather low, but they hoped it would be sufficient to light them to the mouth of the cave. With the aid of a chair they climbed on to the mantelpiece, passed through the door in the panelling to the vaulted chamber, and on into the subterranean passage. They scurried along as fast as they could without stumbling, partly from fear that the candle would go out, and partly in dread lest somebody should be coming from the entrance, and meet them on the way. It was with a feeling of intense relief that, bearing the last guttering scrap of candle, they at length emerged into the daylight.

"Here we are, safe and sound, and met no bogy, thank goodness!" rejoiced Dulcie.

"There's our bogy, waiting!" said Deirdre, pointing to a school hat which suddenly made its appearance from below.

"Gerda, by all that's wonderful!" gasped Dulcie.

Yes, it was Gerda who had followed them, and who now watched them as they came out of the cave. She was paler than usual, and there was a queer set look about her mouth.

"So that was what you wanted the candle for. You might have told me," she remarked.

The two girls began an animated account of their strange adventure. They were so full of it that at the moment it would have been impossible to avoid talking about it. Gerda listened calmly, though she asked one or two questions. She spoke with the constrained manner of one who is putting a strong control on herself.

"So you found nothing to explain the mystery?" she queried.

"Nothing at all. Is it Lillie who's living there and doing her own cooking?"

"And is she a girl or a spook?" added Dulcie.

"Spooks don't drink tea. She must be alive," said Deirdre. "I wonder if Miss Birks knows about her?"

"I guess we'd better not divulge the secret!" chuckled Dulcie. "What would Miss Birks say to us for trespassing in the kitchen-garden?—particularly when she's away."

"We should get into a jolly row!" agreed Deirdre.

"We shall all three get into one as it is if we don't go back quickly," observed Gerda.

Rather conscience-stricken, the chums obeyed her suggestion. They were fortunate enough to slip from the kitchen-garden without being observed, and hoped their escapade would not be discovered. After tea they hurried to make up arrears of practising, but Gerda, evading the vigilance of Mademoiselle, gave an excuse to Miss Harding and absented herself from preparation. Stealing very cautiously from the house she dived through the shrubbery and ran out on to the warren. Casting many a hasty glance behind her to see if she were observed, she hurried along till she reached the little point above St. Perran's well where a rough pile of stones made a natural beacon, easily visible from the sea or from the beach below. Taking her handkerchief from her pocket she tied it to a stick, which she planted at the summit of the pile. Waving in the breeze it was a conspicuous object. She watched it for a moment or two, then walked back along the cliff with the drooping air of one who is almost ready to collapse after meeting a great emergency.

"It was a near thing—a near thing!" she muttered to herself. "Suppose they'd met? Oh, it's too horrible! It was too risky an experiment, really! I hope my danger signal's plain enough. I must get up early to-morrow and take it down before anyone from the school sees it. It'll be difficult with those two in the room—but I'll manage it somehow. Fortunately they're both sound sleepers!"

CHAPTER XVIII

An Alarm

THAT same evening an extraordinary thing happened. It was the custom for glasses of milk, dishes of stewed fruit, and plates of bread and butter to be placed on the table in the dining-hall about eight o'clock. This was done as usual, but when the girls arrived for supper they found a large proportion of the bread and butter had vanished. At first the suspicion fell on Spot, the fox-terrier, but the cook pleaded an alibi on his behalf, proving that he had been in the kitchen the whole time; also, the rifled plates were in the middle of the table, so no dog could have purloined their contents without knocking over glasses, or disturbing spoons and forks.

"I'm afraid it's a two-legged dog," said Miss Harding gravely. "The French window was open, and it would be easy for anyone to walk in and help himself. I'm glad nothing more valuable was taken. I wish Miss Birks were here! It's most unfortunate it should happen on the very evening she's away."

The incident gave cause for serious apprehension. Miss Harding made a most careful round of the house before bedtime, to see that all bolts and shutters were well secured. Though she would not betray her alarm to the girls, she was afraid that a burglary might be committed during the night. Both she and Mademoiselle kept awake till dawn, listening for suspicious footsteps on the gravel outside. All was as usual, however, in the morning; there were no evidences of attempts to force locks or windows, and no trace of the mysterious thief who had taken the bread and butter. Mademoiselle reported indeed that she had again heard the curious sounds which for some nights past had disturbed her. She had risen and patrolled the house, and had come to the unmistakable conclusion that they issued from the barred room. The closed chamber was as much a riddle to teachers as to girls, so Miss Harding merely shook her head, and recommended Mademoiselle to tell her experiences to Miss Birks as soon as the Principal returned.

At five o'clock that afternoon Elyned Hughes came running downstairs with a white, scared face. She solemnly averred that, when passing the door of the mysterious room, she had heard extraordinary noises within.

"It was exactly like somebody moving about and frying sausages. I smelled them too!" she declared.

The report was in part confirmed by several other girls, who pledged their word that they heard stealthy movements when they listened at the barred door.

"Are you absolutely certain, or is it only mice?" queried Gerda. "We've so often fancied things."

"Mice don't clink cans, and strike matches, and clear their throats!" retorted Rhoda.

"But you may have thought it sounded like that."

"I couldn't be mistaken."

"Somebody's there, beyond a doubt," said Agnes.

"Perhaps it's a ghost?" queried Elyned.

"It's nothing supernatural this time, I'll undertake to say—whatever may have made the noises before."

"It ought to be enquired into," declared Doris. "Miss Birks ought to insist on having the bars taken down, and seeing what's going on."

"Oh, no, no! It's best to leave things as they are."

Gerda was looking white and upset and spoke almost hysterically.

"Do you expect the ghost to bolt in amongst us the moment the door is unlocked?" mocked Rhoda.

"No, of course, I'm not so silly! But it's often better to let well alone."

"Mrs. Trevellyan is still away, so Miss Birks couldn't ask her to have the bars taken down now," volunteered Betty Scott.

"So she is," exclaimed Gerda, with an air of relief.

"Ah! You're afraid of the ghost," repeated Rhoda. "I'm more inclined towards the burglar theory. In the circumstances, I think Miss Birks would be quite justified in making an investigation, even without Mrs. Trevellyan's permission."

"I shouldn't wonder myself if Miss Birks called in the police," said Betty Scott.

The girls were in a ferment of excitement over the affair. Deirdre and Dulcie felt that in view of yesterday's discovery they had a strong clue to the mystery. They hesitated as to whether they ought at once to tell Miss Harding, but, as Miss Birks was expected home within an hour or two, they decided it was better to wait till they could deliver their news at head-quarters.

Gerda, during the whole day, had been very abstracted and peculiar in her manner. She was nervous, starting at every sound, and seemed so preoccupied with her own thoughts that she often took no notice when spoken to.

"What's wrong with the Sphinx?" commented Deirdre. "She's absolutely obsessed."

"Yes, I can't make her out. She's disturbed in her mind. That's easy enough to see. There's something queer going on in this school. I hope she's not mixed up in it."

"We'd decidedly better watch her. After all that's happened before, one can't trust her in the least. Until Miss Birks is safely back in the house I feel we oughtn't to let Gerda out of our sight. Who knows what she may be going to do, or whom she's in league with?"

Coupled with the mysterious happenings of last night and to-day, Gerda's palpable uneasiness gave strong grounds for suspicion. The chums watched her like a couple of detectives. They were determined to warn Miss Birks directly on her return. Meanwhile nothing their room-mate did must escape their notice. They were to perform a duet at the musical examination, therefore they had the extreme felicity of doing their practising together. For the same half-hour Gerda was due at the instrument in the next room. They waited to begin until they heard the first bars of her "Arabesque". At the same moment came from the hall the sounds of the bustle occasioned by Miss Birks's arrival home. Deirdre and Dulcie looked at one another in much relief.

"She'll just be downstairs again by the time we've finished practising, and then we'll go straight and tell her," they agreed.

I am afraid neither in the least gave her mind to the piano. Mademoiselle, had she been near, would have been highly irate at the wrong notes and other faults that marred the beauty of their mazurka. Both girls were playing with an ear for the "Arabesque" on the other side of the wall.

"She's stopped!" exclaimed Dulcie, pausing in the middle of a bar. "Now, what's that for, I should like to know? I don't trust you, Miss Gerda Thorwaldson."

But Deirdre was already at the window.

"Look! look!" she gasped. "Gerda's off somewhere!"

The window of the adjacent room was a French one, and the girls could see their schoolfellow open it gently and steal cautiously out on to the lawn. She glanced round to see if she were observed, then ran off in the direction of the kitchen-garden. In a moment the chums had thrown up the sash of their window and followed her. All their old suspicions of her had revived in full force; they were certain she was in league with somebody, and for no good purpose, and they were determined that at last they would unmask her and expose her duplicity. They had spared her before, but this time they intended to act, and act promptly too.

Gerda opened the gate of the kitchen-garden as confidently as if she were not transgressing a rule, and rushed away between the strawberry beds. Pilfering was evidently not her object, for she never even looked at the fruit, but kept straight on towards the end where the horse-radish grew. Keeping her well within sight, the chums went swiftly but cautiously after. She stood for a moment on the piece of waste ground that bounded the cliff, looked carefully round—her pursuers were hidden behind a tree —then plunged down the side of the rock and out of sight. Deirdre and Dulcie each drew a long breath. The conclusion was certain. Without doubt she must be going to pay a visit to the cave which communicated with the mysterious chamber. Whom did she expect to find there?

"To me there's only one course open," declared Deirdre solemnly. "We must go straight to Miss Birks and tell her this very instant."

The Principal, disturbed in the midst of changing her travelling costume, listened with amazement to her insistent pupils' excited account.

"This must be investigated immediately," she declared. "Dulcie, fetch a candle and matches, and you must both accompany me to this cave. You say Gerda has gone on there alone?"

Miss Birks took the affair gravely. She appeared very much concerned, even alarmed. She hurried off at once with the girls to the kitchen-garden.

They led the way down the narrow staircase cut in the cliff, and across the beach and over the rocks. At the entrance to the cave they both uttered a sharp exclamation, for Gerda stood there in an attitude of hesitation, as if unable to make up her mind whether to enter or no. She turned red, and white, and then red again to the tips of her ears when she saw that she was discovered, but she offered no explanation of her presence there. She did not even speak.

"Girls," said Miss Birks, "I think it is highly desirable and necessary that we should follow this passage into the room which I am told is beyond. Deirdre, you go first, with this candle, then Dulcie—Gerda, give me your candle, and walk just in front of me."

Policing the three in the rear, the Principal gave nobody an opportunity to escape. She had her own reasons for her conduct, which at present she did not choose to explain. With a hand on Gerda's shoulder, she forced that unwilling explorer along, and she urged an occasional caution on Deirdre. They had reached the cavern, and now, opening the small inner door, flashed their candles into the room. The result was startling.

On the bed reclined a figure, which, at sight of the light, sprang up with the cry of a hare in a trap—a man, unkempt, ragged, and dirty, bearing the impress of tramp written plainly upon his haggard, unshaven countenance. He darted wildly forward, gazed up at the strangers regarding him, then threw himself on a chair, and buried his face in his hands.

Gerda gave a long sigh of supreme relief. It was evidently not at all what she had expected to see.

"I'm done!" whimpered the tramp. "Send for the bobbies if you like. I'll go quiet."

"You must first tell me what you are doing here," said Miss Birks, stepping down into the room. "Then I can decide whether or no it is necessary to call in the police. Who are you? And where do you come from?"

"I knowed this passage when I was a boy," was the whining reply. "We used to dare each other to go up it, but the door at the end was firm shut. Then when I come back, down on my luck, and without a penny in my pocket to pay for a lodging, I thought I'd at least spend a night there under cover. I'd a bit of candle and a few matches, so I found my way along easy, and there! if the door at the end wasn't broke open, and the place waitin' all ready for me—bed, kettle, cooking-stove, frying-pan, cup and saucer, and all the rest of it, just as if someone 'ad put 'em there a purpose. I wasn't long in takin' possession, and I've lived here five days, and done nobody no harm. I didn't take nothing from the house either, except a bit of bread and butter last night when I felt starving. T'other days I'd found a job on the quay, and was able to buy myself victuals."

"Did you cook sausages?" quavered Dulcie, with intense interest.

"Aye, I'd earned a bit this morning to buy 'em with. Don't know who set up a stove here, but it come in handy for me, all filled ready with oil, too."

"But you know you've no right here," said Miss Birks severely.

"No, mum," reverting to his original whine. "I know that, but I'm a poor man, and I've been unfortunate. I came back to my native place looking for a bit of work. I've bin half over the world since I left it."

"If you're a Pontperran man, somebody ought to be able to vouch for you. What's your name?"

"Abel Galsworthy."

Then Gerda sprang forward with intense, irrepressible excitement on her face.

"Not Abel Galsworthy who was at one time under-gardener at the Castle?" she queried eagerly.

"The same—at your service, miss."

"And you were dismissed for—for——"

"For borrowing a matter of a few pears, that made a little disagreement betwixt me and the head gardener. I swore I'd try another line of life, and I shipped as a fireman on board a steamer bound for America, and worked my way over the continent to California. I didn't get on with the Yankees, so I took a turn to Australia, but that didn't suit me no better, and after I'd knocked about till I was tired of it, I come home."

"Do you remember that when you were at the Castle you witnessed a paper that the old Squire signed?"

"Aye, I remember it as if it was yesterday. Me and Jim Robinson, the under-groom, was the witnesses, but Jim's been gone this many a year."

"Should you know your own handwriting again? Could you swear to it?"

"I'd take my Bible oath afore a judge and jury, if need be."

"Then—oh! thank Heaven I have pieced the broken link of my chain!" cried Gerda. "Oh! can I really clear my father's name at last, and wipe the stain from the honour of the Trevellyans?"

"What does she mean?" asked Dulcie. "I don't understand!"

"It's all a jig-saw puzzle to me!" said Deirdre. "What does Gerda know about the Castle, and the old Squire, and a paper? And what has she to do with the honour of the Trevellyans?"

"I guessed the riddle long ago," smiled Miss Birks, laying a friendly hand on Gerda's arm. "The likeness to Ronnie was enough to tell me that she was his sister."

CHAPTER XIX

A Torn Letter

IN order to understand the events which were happening at the Dower House we must go back for a period of some years in the history of the family at the Castle. The late owner, Squire Trevellyan, having lost his only child, had practically adopted his nephew L'Estrange Trevellyan as his heir. He had indeed other nephews and nieces, but they were the children of his sisters, and it seemed to him fitting that L'Estrange, the only one who bore the family name of Trevellyan, should inherit his Cornish estate. The young fellow was an immense favourite with his uncle and aunt, they regarded him in the light of a son, the Castle was considered his home, and they had even decided upon an alliance for him with the daughter of a neighbouring baronet. But in this matter L'Estrange had defied the wishes of the autocratic old squire, and, making his own choice, had wedded a lady of less aristocratic birth. His marriage caused a great coolness between himself and his uncle and aunt; his bride was not asked to the Castle nor openly recognized, and he was given to understand that he had seriously injured his chances of succession to the estate. His cousins, who had long been jealous of his prospects, were not slow to avail themselves of this opportunity, and did all they could to make mischief and to widen the breach.

Matters went on thus for about ten years, during which time, though Squire and Mrs. Trevellyan occasionally asked L'Estrange to the Castle, they still refused to have anything to do with his wife, and did not see either of his children. At the Squire's death there was great anxiety among the relatives to know how he had disposed of his property. When the will was read it was found that he had left the Castle and entire estate to his wife, with power to bequeath it as she wished, and equal money legacies to all his nephews and nieces; but at the end came a codicil revoking the former part of the will, leaving only small legacies to the other nephews and nieces, but a large sum to L'Estrange, and bequeathing the Castle and property to him after Mrs. Trevellyan's death. The relations, furiously angry to be thus cut out, disputed the validity of the codicil. There were many points in its disfavour. The lawyer who had drawn it up was dead, and of the two witnesses who had signed their names to it one was missing and the other dead. There was therefore not a solitary person left to vouch for it. The family decided to go to law, and in the case which followed the handwriting experts decided that the signature to the codicil was not genuine, giving it as their opinion that it had been forged by L'Estrange Trevellyan.

The case against L'Estrange looked extremely black, for he had been staying at the Castle at the time of his uncle's illness and death. In view of the decision in the case a criminal charge of forgery was laid against him, and a warrant issued for his arrest. Before it was out, however, he had disappeared—no one knew whither.

To Mrs. Trevellyan the evidence seemed overwhelming, and in spite of her great affection for her nephew, she believed him guilty. It had always been her great wish that the Castle and estate should pass to one who bore the name of Trevellyan, and at this dreadful crisis she offered to adopt L'Estrange's little son, and to bring him up as heir to the property. Her one condition was that she must have the child absolutely, and that his father and mother should not attempt in any way to obtain access to him. In his desperate circumstances L'Estrange had consented; the boy was handed over to his great-aunt, and had been brought up at the Castle without any remembrance of his own home and parents.

The affair had, of course, made a great stir in the neighbourhood, but as L'Estrange had not remained in the country to face a prosecution, and therefore no trial of the case had followed, opinions were divided as to his guilt. In the course of five years the excitement had died down, and though the story was well known at Pontperran it was regarded as the Trevellyan family skeleton, and best buried in oblivion. Miss Birks had tried to keep the matter from her pupils; they had a vague knowledge that Ronnie's father was unsatisfactory, but they had been able to glean no further details. In view, however, of the strange chain of events which had just transpired, Miss Birks gave Deirdre and Dulcie, in private, a hasty outline of the circumstances, telling them that Gerda was in reality the daughter of Mr. L'Estrange Trevellyan, and that from certain evidence which she had been able to collect she was confident of disproving the charge which had been brought against her father.

Though the chums were thus briefly in possession of their school-mate's secret, they felt there were many pieces in the puzzle which they could not yet fit together. When they went to bed that night they begged Gerda to give them a full and complete explanation. To their surprise she immediately consented; indeed, instead of keeping her old habit of reserve she seemed anxious to take them into her confidence and to pour her whole story into their listening ears.

"If you're Ronnie's sister you can't be Gerda Thorwaldson," said Dulcie. "I didn't know Ronnie had a sister. I thought he was an only child."

"There are just the two of us," replied Gerda. "I am nine years older than he is, so I've always felt almost like a mother to him. Shall I tell you everything? Quite from the beginning? Miss Harding will excuse us for talking to-night. When our terrible trouble came upon us Ronnie was only fifteen months old—such a darling! He could just walk and say little words. I have his photo inside my work-box. You can imagine the grief it was to part with him, our baby, who'd never been a day from us. Mother was very brave—she realized that she had to decide between Father and her boy, and of course she chose Father. We knew it was entirely for Ronnie's good. Mrs. Trevellyan would bring him up in the old family home as an English boy should be, and would make him her heir; and we could only take him from one foreign place to another, and give him nothing but poverty and a tarnished name. You know, of course, that my father was accused of having forged a codicil to his uncle, Squire Trevellyan's will. By a round of misfortune everything seemed to combine in his disfavour. One witness to the codicil was dead, the other was missing, and though advertisements were put in the papers offering a reward for news of his whereabouts he could not be found. Mr. Forster, the lawyer who had drawn up both the will and the codicil, was dead, so there was no evidence on Father's side, and the case went heavily against him.

"The codicil having been disproved, the public prosecutor stepped in and issued a warrant to arrest my father on a charge of forgery. In the circumstances, with no witnesses obtainable, it was not considered wise for him to stand the doubtful chance of a trial, and acting on the advice of his best friends, though very much against his own wishes, he quietly left the country. For nearly five years he, Mother, and I have lived together in various continental towns, constantly moving on, as we feared the foreign police might recognize the description circulated at the time of his escape and arrest him under an extradition warrant. For safety we changed our name at almost every place. I cannot express the wretched uncertainty and the misery of this hunted life, especially when we knew the charge to be so utterly false. There would have been only one worse evil—to see him wrongfully sentenced and sent to a convict prison. The dread of that possible horror we endured from day to day. Meantime Mother, though she would not confess it, fretted terribly at Ronnie's loss. As year after year went by, and she pictured him growing older, it became harder and harder for her to exist without hearing the least word about him.

"'If I had even one poor little snapshot photo it would comfort me,' she said once. 'It would show me my darling is well and happy and cared for in his new home.'

"Then an idea came to me. Though I had never been at Pontperran in my life I had often heard my father speak of the Dower House, and I knew it was close to the Castle. I begged to be sent to school there, for I thought I should find some opportunity of seeing Ronnie, and not only taking a photo of him, but sending first-hand news about him to Mother. I hoped also—but it seemed such a forlorn hope!—that if I were on the spot I might pick up some information that might throw a light on the case and help to clear my father's honour. There seemed little risk of my being detected, for Mrs. Trevellyan had never seen me—Aunt Edith, I ought to call her—and I meant to keep carefully out of her way.

"Mother jumped at my suggestion. I could see that the mere chance of news of Ronnie put fresh life into her, and after some persuasion Father agreed to let me go. I took the name of Gerda Thorwaldson, and the letters to Miss Birks, arranging for me to be received as a pupil, were written from Donnerfest, a little town in Germany. Mother brought me to London, and put me safely into the train for Cornwall. Then she used the opportunity of being in England to pay quiet visits to some of her own relations whom she had not seen for many years.

"My father had a friend, a man who believed in his innocence, and did his best to help him. This Mr. Carr took him a cruise on his yacht, and came to Cornish waters, tacking about the coast from Avonporth to Kergoff. By borrowing the yacht's dinghy, Father was able sometimes to land near Portperran and meet me for a few minutes. Of course it was a terribly risky thing to do, for he was liable to be arrested any moment that he set his foot on English soil; but he longed so much to see me, and, above all, to hear what I could tell of Ronnie. He was so anxious to catch a glimpse of the little fellow for himself that he insisted upon venturing farther on shore. He knew the secret of the barred room, so, bringing with him an oil cooking-stove, a kettle, and a few other things from the yacht, he took up his quarters there for a while.

"I was in an agony lest he should be discovered. I cannot tell you what I suffered on this account. He did not stay the whole time at the cave; indeed he lived mostly on the yacht, but kept spending occasional nights in the secret room. I never knew whether he was there or not, and the uncertainty made me wretched.

"During the last five years we had seemed continually to be standing on the brink of a volcano, and I was always prepared to face the worst.

"I can scarcely express how deeply I realized the difference between myself and all the other girls at school. I know you thought me reserved and uncommunicative and stand-off and everything that is disagreeable, but I simply dared not talk, for fear I might reveal something that would betray my father. You with your happy homes, and nothing to conceal, how can you understand what it is perpetually to guard a dreadful secret? I could tell you nothing about my home, for we had no home, we had only moved on from one lodging to another, and left no address behind. I could see that you misjudged me, and were full of suspicions, but I could not explain.

"You were annoyed with me for winning favour with Ronnie. You would not have grudged me his affection if you had known how I had craved for him all these years, and how hard, how very hard it was to be obliged to treat him as if I were an entire stranger, instead of his own sister. Then I was terribly afraid of meeting Mrs. Trevellyan, lest she should recognize my likeness to my father and guess our secret. I avoided her on every possible occasion, and on the whole I managed very successfully to keep out of her way.

"But Mother was pining and yearning to see Ronnie. The little photos I had sent, and my descriptions of him, added to the fact of her being in England, so near to him, only made her long for him more bitterly than before. It seemed so cruel that she—his own mother—must be so utterly parted from him. I was determined that she should have at least the poor satisfaction of seeing him, and I plotted and schemed to contrive a meeting. I decided that on the night of the beacon fire I might manage to carry Ronnie away for a few minutes, so as to give the opportunity we wanted. I cajoled him with promises of fairies, and persuaded him quite easily to go with me to find them. Father, who was as anxious and excited as Mother, was waiting with a boat, but you know the rest, for you followed us. Perhaps Mrs. Trevellyan suspected something—she must have known shortly afterwards, for she recognized Father when he rescued Ronnie on the cliff. I heard her call him by his name. Father used to be her favourite nephew, indeed he was almost like a son to her, but she had believed him guilty, and had told him never to show his face to her again. Even before Squire Trevellyan's death there had already been an estrangement between them because of his marriage. My mother was not their choice, and on this account Mrs. Trevellyan objected to her, and only once consented to meet her. Though Father sometimes went to the Castle to visit his uncle and aunt, my mother and I were never invited there, and Mrs. Trevellyan had not seen Ronnie until she adopted him.

"After the beacon fire I felt I had accomplished one part at least of my mission at school. Mother had seen and kissed her boy, and she seemed a little comforted and cheered in consequence. But the greater task which I had set myself, that of clearing my father's name, was still untouched. One possible clue there was which I thought I might follow up. Do you remember how in February we went to Forster's Folly? I knew that Mr. Forster had been the lawyer who drew up Squire Trevellyan's will and the famous codicil. That was the reason why I was so anxious to go into the house, and so excited when we found those letters lying about upstairs. I would have stayed to look at them if I had dared. You Deirdre, tore off a scrap of a letter with a crest on it, to take for your collection. Now that crest was the boar's head of the Trevellyans, which I knew very well, for it used to be on our own note-paper before our trouble came. You had torn the piece from the rest of the letter, but I could read—

"'DEAR FORST ..

"'Kindly c.....'

And on turning the scrap over I found on the other side—

"'wish to ...

"'extra codi......'

"Could it be possible, I speculated, that this was a portion of an original letter sent by Squire Trevellyan to Mr. Forster, asking him to come to the house, as he wished to make an extra codicil to his will? If that were really so, it would make a most important piece of evidence. I begged you to give me the crest, but you would not part with it then, and locked it up. I was most anxious to go to Forster's Folly again and try to find the rest of the letter, but I never found an opportunity until last week. It was too far to venture in our recreation time, and I dare not be absent from school for hours without leave. I would have told Mother and asked her to go, but there were two reasons against this. We feared she might be known to the police, and that they would watch her so as to obtain some clue to my father's whereabouts, so she did not wish to venture into Cornwall while he was near the coast. When she came to see Ronnie she went over first to France, and our friend fetched her from there in the yacht, and took her back to St. Malo, so that she need not be seen on the South-Western Railway.

"My second reason was that until I could be sure that the other part of the letter really contained what I expected, it seemed cruel to raise false hopes. If you had seen, as I have, the bitter, bitter tragedy of my parents' lives, you would understand how I wanted to spare them a disappointment. So I waited and waited, and at last my opportunity came. Circumstances were kind, and when we had our whole day's holiday, I was chosen as a hare. Oh, how rejoiced I was when you decided to go past the windmill to Kergoff! I was determined to put in a visit somehow to the old house, but it came so naturally when we needed more paper. To my intense delight I found the other portion of the letter that I wanted, and then you were kind and gave me the scrap with the crest. The two fit exactly together. Look, I will show you! This is what they make when joined—

"'THE CASTLE,

"'*Thursday.*

"'DEAR FORSTER,

"'Kindly come to-morrow morning about eleven, if you can make that convenient, as I want to consult you on a matter of some importance. Those Victoria Mine shares have gone up beyond my wildest dreams, and I'm thinking of selling out now, and clearing what I can. They'll make a difference to my estate, and to meet this I wish to add an extra codicil to my will. L'Estrange is here, so you will see him. I have not been well—a touch of the old heart trouble, I am afraid. I must ask Jones to arrange for me to consult a London specialist. If you cannot come to-morrow morning, please arrange Saturday.

"'Sincerely yours,

"'RICHARD TREVELLYAN.'

This is very strong evidence that Squire Trevellyan intended making the codicil to his will. I am longing to show it to Father and Mother, but they are both away cruising in the yacht. I don't know where they are now; they promised to send me word when it was safe for me to write to them.

"When we began to hear those strange noises in the barred room, and yesterday you discovered the secret of its entrance, I was dreadfully alarmed. I thought my father must have come back again in spite of my warnings that the cave was unsafe. I felt so nervous and uneasy that at last I decided to go and see for myself, and beg him not to stay.

"When I reached the entrance, however, I did not dare to go in alone, in case it should be somebody else instead of my father who was there. I reproached myself for my cowardice, but I was only just screwing my courage to the point when you two arrived with Miss Birks. I need not tell you how relieved I was when we did not find my father. You saw my frantic excitement when it turned out that the tramp whom we discovered was no other than Abel Galsworthy, the missing witness to the will? With his oath and this precious, precious letter the evidence ought to be complete. Oh, the rapture of the day when Father's name is cleared and his honour restored, and he can live anywhere he likes, openly and without fear. Now I have told you my whole story. I'm sure you'll see why I was so queer and secretive, and so different from other girls."

"We understand and sympathize now," said Deirdre, "but you puzzled us very much at the time."

"We thought you were a German spy," chuckled Dulcie. "We were going to get great credit by finding out your wicked plot against England, and informing the Government!"

"Had you anything to do with that man in the aeroplane? Why, I'd almost forgotten him!" exclaimed Deirdre.

"I never even knew there was an aeroplane here," protested Gerda.

"You haven't told us your real name yet," urged Dulcie.

"Mary Gerda Trevellyan. Father and Mother have always called me Mamie, but I like Gerda best, and when I came to school I begged to be 'Gerda Thorwaldson', so that part at least of my name was genuine."

"Weren't you afraid that Mrs. Trevellyan might discover you through that?"

"She had always heard me alluded to as Mamie. We thought she had probably quite forgotten the 'Gerda'."

"There's one thing I still can't understand," said Dulcie. "We found out the entrance to the barred room, but why was it ever barred? It seems so extraordinary—right in the middle of a school."

"I can explain that too," returned Gerda. "Father has often told me the story. Years and years ago Squire and Mrs. Trevellyan had one only child, a little girl named Lillie. Father was very fond of this cousin, and they were almost like brother and sister together. Then, when she was ten years old, she died. At that time they were living at the Dower House, because alterations were being made at the Castle. Her death was very sudden—she was only ill a few hours. One day she was laughing and playing about, and on the next she was dead. Her poor father and mother were simply heart-broken. They took her toys, and all her little treasures, and put them in her bedroom, which they left just as if she were going to occupy it still. Then they locked up the door and barred it, and declared that during their lifetime nobody should ever enter. It was to be sacred to Lillie, and no one else must use it. My father, of course, knew about it, and he also knew of the secret passage—an old smuggler's way—that led into it from the cave. The door of this passage had been carefully nailed up before Lillie used the room, but he had heard that it opened over the fireplace. In his desperate need of a safe shelter he remembered this place, came up the passage, then forced the door and found his way into the room. He said it was surely no crime, for 'little Cousin Lillie' had been fond of him, and always ready to screen him in his boyish days, so he thought, if she could know, she would be glad for him to use what had once been hers."

"I haven't asked half all yet," persisted Dulcie. "Do you remember when first you came to school, we all tried our luck at St. Perran's well, and you were the only one who did the right things, and whose stick floated away? How did you manage it?"

Gerda smiled.

"Father had often told me about the well, and the exact way to perform St. Perran's ceremony. He used to try it with Lillie when he was a little boy. He said half the secret was to unstop the channel above the spring. My wish was that I might clear his name, so you see it came true, though at the time it seemed as unlikely as flying in an aeroplane to America."

"You put a message in a bottle and threw it into the sea for your father," said Deirdre. "You didn't know Dulcie and I fished it out?"

"Oh! Did you?" said Gerda reproachfully. "Then that was the letter he never received?"

Gerda's discovery in Abel Galsworthy of the missing witness for whom such long search had been made was certainly a very fortunate circumstance for that worthy. Instead of being handed over to the police, and prosecuted for trespassing and pilfering, he found himself provided with new clothes, comfortably lodged in the village, and given a promise of work when his important part in the law proceedings should be over. At present he was the hero of the hour, for on his word alone hung Mr. Trevellyan's honour. As the other witness and the lawyer were both dead, his oath to his signature would be sufficient to prove the genuineness of the codicil. There were, of course, elaborate legal proceedings to be taken. Mr. Trevellyan appealed for a reversal of the judgment in the former trial, and the case would have to wait its turn before it could come before the court. As the warrant for his arrest was still technically in force, he was obliged to continue living on the yacht until his innocence had been officially recognized—a state of affairs that greatly roused Gerda's indignation, though Miss Birks preached patience.

"I wanted Father and Mother to come to the prize-giving," she lamented.

"These legal difficulties cannot be rolled away in a few days," said Miss Birks. "Let us be thankful that we can count upon success later on."

Now that Gerda no longer needed to hide a tragic secret, her whole behaviour at the Dower House had altered, and her schoolfellows hardly recognized in the merry, genial, sociable companion, which she now proved, the silent recluse who had given her confidence to nobody. In this fresh attitude she was highly popular; the romance of her story appealed to the girls, and they were anxious to make up to her for having misjudged her. Also they greatly appreciated her newly-discovered capacity for fun and humour.

"Gerda never made one solitary joke before, and now she keeps us laughing all day," said Betty Scott.

"How could she laugh when she was carrying that terrible burden all the time?" commented Jessie Macpherson. "Poor child! No wonder she's different now the shadow's removed from her life."

"We'll have ripping fun with her next term," anticipated Annie Pridwell.

Meanwhile very little of the old term was left. The dreaded examination week arrived, bringing Dr. Harvey James to test those who were to undergo the piano ordeal, and Mr. Leonard Pearce to criticize the artistic efforts. In the other subjects there were written papers, which were corrected and judged by the donors of the prizes. In spite of much apprehension on the part of the girls, Dr. Harvey James made a good impression, and did not turn out to be the strict martinet they expected; indeed he commented so kindly and so helpfully on their playing that they began to look forward to their lessons with him during the forthcoming autumn.

The art class spent a delightful though anxious afternoon, sketching a group of picturesque Eastern pots artistically grouped by Mr. Leonard Pearce, who was kind and charitable in his criticisms of their little exhibition of paintings hung in the big classroom. To their delight he finished his visit by himself making a study of the pots, while they stood round and watched his clever brush dabbing on the colour with swift and skilful strokes.

"Miss Birks is going to have his sketch framed," said Deirdre appreciatively, when he had gone.

"I wish he could teach us every week," declared the art enthusiasts.

"Ah! you see, he lives in London, and only comes to Cornwall sometimes for a holiday. But Miss Birks has promised to get an artist next summer to give us sketching lessons."

One advantage of the smallness of the school was that it was not a lengthy matter to correct the examination papers of only twenty pupils. That work was soon over, and the girls had not long to remain in suspense before the lists were ready. The annual prize-giving was always the occasion of a social gathering. Some of the girls' parents came down for it, and friends in the neighbourhood were invited. If the weather were favourable, it was generally held in the garden, and this time, the sky being cloudless, all arrangements had been made on the lawn, where the gardener had erected a temporary platform. It seemed a great day to Gerda, as she came downstairs in her white dress, and watched the company that was already beginning to arrive. If only her father and mother could have been numbered among the guests her bliss would have been complete. Ronnie, however, was running in and out like a sunbeam, and her aunt had spoken to her, and had been kindness itself.

"We must all let bygones be bygones now, my dear, and rejoice together at this happy ending of our troubles," said Mrs. Trevellyan. "I hope you will soon come to know the Castle as well as Ronnie does, and feel equally at home there."

Most of the prizes fell exactly as had been expected. Jessie Macpherson won the lion's share in the Sixth, Hilda Marriott scored the record for VA, and Barbara Marshall and Romola Harvey divided the honours of VB. Deirdre got "highly commended" for both music and drawing, but Dulcie, despite her valorous spurt at the finish, had no luck. She was only too delighted, however, to find that the prize for which she had tried—that for general improvement—had been awarded to Gerda.

"She deserves it if anyone does," she whispered to Deirdre. "I say, dare we start three cheers for her?"

"We'll risk it," returned Deirdre, augmenting the applause by a vigorous "Hip-hip-hip hooray!" which was at once taken up by the entire school. Gerda, red as a rose, walked back from the platform, blushing now with real bashfulness, instead of her old nervous apprehension. Ronnie was waving his little hat and shouting the shrillest of cheers, and Mrs. Trevellyan was clapping her best.

"Ave! Ave! winner of General Improvement!" exclaimed the members of VB, as they welcomed her back to their particular bench. "Miss Birks couldn't have given it better!"

Gerda's eyes filled with tears.

"I'm glad if you do find me improved," she said. "It's ever so nice of you to be kind to me now. I was horrid before—and I knew it—but I couldn't help it."

"We understand exactly," sympathized the girls.

There is very little more of our story left to be told. Mr. Trevellyan won his case, and successfully proved his innocence to the whole world. Restored to good name and fortune, he has taken "Overdale", a pretty house in the neighbourhood of Pontperran, which happened to be to let. Gerda continues a pupil at the Dower House, though she is often able to visit her own home. Ronnie, while he will see his aunt every day, is to live with his parents, a fitting and also a very salutary arrangement, for he is no longer a baby, and was growing too much for Mrs. Trevellyan's and Miss Herbert's powers of management. The self-willed little fellow respects his father's authority, and will run far less risk of getting spoilt than when he was "King of the Castle".

"In a year or two the young rascal will be old enough for school," said Mr. Trevellyan, "and in the meantime he must get to know his mother and me."

Gerda is immensely delighted with her new home, and very proud to take school friends there on half-holidays. Deirdre and Dulcie are frequent visitors. Abel Galsworthy, a reformed character after his wanderings, is gardener at Overdale, and likely to prove a most devoted servant; and as for the torn letter, it is framed and glazed, and occupies the place of honour on the wall over the chimney-piece in Gerda's bedroom.

CPSIA information can be obtained
at www.ICGtesting.com
Printed in the USA
BVHW03s0137100518
515873BV00007B/37/P